COPYCAT

RECIPES

A Step-by-Step Cookbook to Easily Making the Most Popular and Tasty Dishes of Famous Restaurants and Fast Food at Home

ASIA STONE

Table of Contents

INTRODUCTION

Your favorite meals are right at your fingertips!

At this very moment, more so than ever before, we have had to actively stay at home. When the world came to a halt at the start of 2020, a lot of us were not only *bored in the house*; we also lacked the freedom to go out to our favorite restaurants and order whatever we craved at that very moment. With that luxury of choice coming to a halt, that meant that we now had no choice but to face up to our one fear: the dreaded kitchen! The part of our house that we so often look past. We'd only ever glance over at it when the dishes needed to be attended to or to check if the milk had gone off.

Well, instead of perceiving the kitchen as a chore-ground, our aim here at Copycat is to help you start to perceive your kitchen as a playground! A playground filled with endless possibilities, where you can travel the world through cuisine and their flavors. Through our carefully curated cookbook, you'll be able to visit the flavors of Thai-style stir-fry, and then the very next day, you can hop on a jet to Italy to experience the gloriously divine pastas, pestos, and pizzas that Italy has blessed us with. But it doesn't stop there—there's Indian cuisine and Portuguese seafood stews, and you might even take a visit down to South Africa for their famous custardy dessert. Expect to become one of the "cool kids" (which you always were a part of!) and hop on the trend train of desserts and milkshakes that were sparked by Instagram challenges. Then take a little cruise to one of your favorite drive-thru restaurants to pick up some of your favorite Chicago-style deep dish pizza!

What is the best part about this all, you may ask?

You can enjoy this whole journey from the comfort of your own home! Not to mention the cost efficiency of it all. Once you get the hang of making a few of your favorite recipes, you'll soon find out how much cheaper home-cooked meals are. Not to mention, you yield much more for that money's worth, and you'll also start to add your own little unique touches to the recipes, making them your own. It's something that money definitely can't buy.

Are you excited to go on this journey and explore the world with us, here at Copycat?

If you are, consider leaving us a review on how you found your journey through this cookbook, and if we helped you travel to all of your favorite restaurants (and further)! Let us know what recipes you chose to tackle and how they turned out–this is our journey and we'd love to hear your experience with us!

Throughout the process of curating this list, we've also incorporated a "Difficulty Level" so that you can also see how challenging and time consuming the recipe might be. Thus, we've aimed to make this cookbook an all-inclusive one, covering not only a diverse range of copycat recipes but also inclusive of all levels of cooking skills. Whether you're a beginner who might have accidentally once set popcorn on fire or a chef in the making–there is at least one recipe for each and every one of our readers to start with.

The difficulty levels are based on a scale of 1-10:

1. Extremely easy. Not much effort or time required to prepare this dish.
2. Minimal effort required to prepare this dish. This will usually consist of preparation tasks such as washing and cutting vegetables or blending a few ingredients together.
3. While it might still be easy to prepare, you might have to switch the stove on for 2 minutes.
4. An average amount of time and effort spent. This is usually for meals between 30 minutes to an hour in total.
5. Still maintaining an average amount of effort and time. You might start to work more with the stove and/or oven.
6. Start to pay close attention to the ingredients and methods in play. While this level might still be average, you're starting to work a lot more with flavors and how they work with other ingredients.
7. You might start to tackle more than one pot/pan at a time. There might be preparation/marinating to be done prior to cooking. The recipe might still be simple, but it's a little more time consuming.

8. Certain techniques are brought in to make the dish more unique and special. This level will start rating more complex dishes from overseas such as your seafood and red meat meals (the meals that you might make if you want to impress someone on a fancy date night).
9. Pay close attention to the ingredients and methods used. These recipes might require meticulous work from your end.
10. There's only one bad-boy recipe that made it to the top (and you'll have to keep reading to find out which one it is). If you manage to tackle this challenge, you'll definitely be reaping some pretty delicious rewards!

The exciting factor that these "difficulty levels" offer you as the reader is, firstly, the opportunity to dip your toe in the water, if you're a beginner. You can start with the easier recipes and work your way up the ladder. A lot of the time, what can throw a person off cooking is simply that they've found a recipe that might be too overwhelming for their level of expertise at the time. As the cheesy saying goes: practice makes perfect, and that's what this difficulty level guideline will help you with!

The difficulty levels will also help you to gain a better understanding of what you can make within your given resources: time restraints, your level of skill, and the effort required. Some days we might be feeling a little lazier than other days (or you might even be feeling a little sick); this difficulty rating will help you to find a recipe that's perfectly suited to your condition.

Lastly, this difficulty level rating will hopefully encourage you to take on more challenges and expand your horizons. It will hopefully serve as a motivational tool for you to continue growing, learning, and challenging yourself in regard to what you can prepare in the kitchen. It should boost your morale that you've built up, and you will now be excited to prepare some awesome and delicious meals for yourself and others.

With that being said, get ready for the journey, as we're now fully prepared to take off! And the best part about this journey is that you get to choose where we're headed, and we'll help get you there!

Please enjoy our cookbook; hopefully it inspires and motivates you to take on some of your favorite meals. Don't forget to leave a review if you're enjoying the journey so far!

Chapter One

APPETIZERS & SNACKS

First thing's first–appetizers and snacks, always! These light meals, finger foods, or entrees–whatever nickname you'd like to call them–serve a much more important role than simply looking cute on the dinner table (which is definitely still a very important factor, let's not forget the cute tiny food aesthetics). Appetizers and snacks actually help us to open up our stomachs to receive bigger meals. It helps us to not only curb our hunger, but it also stops us from overeating main meals, because we think that we might still be hungry enough for that second serving. While second servings are great (especially if the food is impeccable), overeating is quite a common issue that we constantly overlook because our stomachs haven't had time to process the food before we're getting up for another round. Snacks and appetizers serve that specific purpose: to regulate our stomachs so that when it is time for our main meals, we're not starving nor do we find ourselves overeating. Along with this advantage, we can also experience a lethargic feeling due to overeating or eating too quickly. What appetizers and snacks do is provide you with a good and constant flow of energy that's in your favor. It will keep you light and energized so that you can reach your mealtimes and eat a good portion's worth of a main meal.

In this chapter, we'll cover five very different forms of appetizers (that can also act as snacks). Some are meaty, some are cheesy, and some are spicy! These appetizers are curated more towards entertaining guests or simply enjoying a lovely comfort snack. There is a healthy option within the list, but what appetizers mainly aim to do is incorporate bread/carbs into the recipe so that your stomach is nicely lined for a main course; therefore, quite a few of these options include some form of carbohydrate.

The recipes that we'll touch on in this chapter are cheesy pastry sticks, glazed chicken wings, garlic toasts, jalapeño poppers, and a very interesting but delicious tarte soleil (which is a French-inspired dish that essentially is a pull-apart pastry). The options are as diverse as they can get and are all equally tantalizing and delicious. So, without further ado, let's dive into our first recipe.

OVEN BAKED CHEESE TWISTS

Whether you're in the mood for a cheesy snack or looking for a quick bite to keep your guests entertained, crispy, cheesy bites are always a great option to consider. These salty, flaky pastries are quick to make and the perfect balance of crunch and melted cheese.

Difficulty Level: 3
Preparation Time: 15 minutes
Cooking Time: 15-18 minutes
Total Time: 40 minutes

Nutritional Info Per Serving Servings: 14 cheese sticks	
Calories	233 calories
Carbohydrates	16.1g
Fat	16.1g
Protein	6.6g

Estimated Budget: $7.00

Ingredients:

- 1 packet of frozen puff pastry (preferably 14 ounces). **Note**: defrost prior to using.

- All-purpose flour, just a pinch to lightly coat your surface
- 6 ounces of semifirm cheese (preferably Parmesan, but this is to your preference)
- 1 large egg yolk
- 1 tsp of water
- 1 tsp of paprika, divided in half
- ¼ tsp of cayenne pepper
- A pinch of chili flakes (optional)
- Salt & black pepper to taste
- A sprinkle of mixed herbs

Note: A sprinkle of Feta cheese can be mixed in with the other cheese, if you're looking for something more flavorful!

Instructions:

1. Set your oven to preheat at 400°F.
2. Grate the 6 ounces of cheese of your choice through the medium side of your grater.
3. Get out 2 baking sheets and layer them with parchment paper (alternatively, you can spray the sheets with cooking spray).
4. Lightly coat a working surface with flour and roll out your puff pastry with a rolling pin.
5. Separate the puff pastry if it comes in 2 layers; if it doesn't, cut the pastry in half, then roll again to flatten the pastry out.

6. In a small bowl, mix together the egg yolk with the 1 tsp of water. Evenly brush half of the mixture onto one side of one of the pastry layers.

7. Sprinkle half of the grated cheese onto the egg-washed pastry layer (you can sprinkle in the Feta cheese/mix of other cheeses if you'd like variety).

8. Evenly sprinkle the ½-teaspoon paprika and cayenne pepper over the cheese, then season with salt, pepper, and mixed herbs.

9. Place the non-egg-washed layer over the cheese layer and gently press the layer down. Egg wash this top layer with the remaining mixture.

10. Sprinkle the remaining cheese, paprika, salt, and pepper on the top layer.

11. Lightly coat your rolling pin with more flour and roll the layers out into about ¼ inch in thickness (try to aim for a rectangular-resembling shape).

12. Cut the pastry into strips with each strip about ½ an inch in thickness.

13. Pinch either ends of one strip and twirl it a few times then lay it down on the baking tray. Repeat the process with the rest of the strips, leaving a small space between each strip on the baking trays.

14. Pop the cheese twirls in the oven and bake for 12-18 minutes until golden brown.

15. You can sprinkle more salt over the top of the cheese twirls if you enjoy more of a salty snack. Serve warm.

RICOTTA, BROCCOLI, & HONEY TOASTS

For a healthier snack option, this divine mix of ricotta cheese, garlic, broccoli, and honey is quick to whip up, a fantastic snack, and bursting with flavor!

Difficulty Level: 2
Preparation Time: 10 minutes
Cooking Time: 20 minutes
Total Time: 30 minutes

Nutritional Info Per Serving **Servings:** 12 slices of toast	
Calories	307
Carbohydrates	42g
Fat	10.7g
Protein	11.9g

Estimated Budget: $6.00

Ingredients:

- 1 French baguette, sliced (around 12 slices)
- 6 tsps of extra virgin olive oil, divided
- 1 head of garlic, separate the cloves

- 1 head of broccoli, florets chopped into ½" pieces
- 1 tbsp of honey
- 1 tsp of white wine vinegar
- ½ tsp of crushed red chili flakes
- 1 ½ cups of fresh ricotta
- Salt & pepper to taste

Instructions:

1. Preheat your oven to 400°F and set racks on the upper and lower third of the oven.
2. On a baking sheet, lay out the baguette slices and drizzle 2 tbsps of olive oil over them. Shake the baking sheet around so that the oil mixes well with the bread slices and then rearrange the slices so that they're evenly laid out.
3. On another baking sheet, lay out your broccoli florets and garlic cloves, then drizzle with the remaining 4 tbsps of oil. Season well with salt and pepper, then toss on the baking sheet to combine the ingredients. Note: if you're worried about tossing the contents on the baking sheet, you can always place them in a bowl and mix; the above instruction is only to reduce the number of dirty dishes you'll have to deal with later!
4. Pop the baking sheet with broccoli on the top rack of the oven and the baking sheet with bread on the bottom rack. Bake the bread for about 10-12 minutes, until golden brown. Keep the broccoli in for about 15-20 minutes until the

broccoli is nice and tender. Allow the contents to cool.

5. While the contents are in the oven, combine honey, vinegar, and the red chili flakes in a small bowl. Whisk well, until the ingredients are well combined.

6. Once the garlic cloves have cooled off, squeeze them out of their skins and place in another small bowl. Mash with a spoon (or if you have a pestle and mortar, this is ideal), until the cloves turn into a paste. Season the mix with salt, pepper, and ricotta, then mix well to infuse the ingredients.

7. Use the ricotta mix as a spread and evenly layer it over each toasted slice. Then layer on your roasted broccoli and drizzle with the honey mixture. For an extra kick, you can sprinkle more chili flakes onto the slices (it's great for a light summer's snack)!

CHEESY JALAPEÑO POPPERS

If you're looking for a spicy, cheesy, and crumbed snack, jalapeño poppers will definitely satisfy that craving! Poppers are a great entertainment snack, especially if you're hosting a get-together with a few drinks. Similar to the honey & ricotta toast, these cheesy jalapeño poppers are an exciting, flavorful experience with every bite taken!

Difficulty Level: 3
Preparation Time: 45 minutes
Cooking Time: 15 minutes
Total Time: 1 hour

Nutritional Info Per Serving Servings: 20 poppers	
Calories	134
Carbohydrates	5.7g
Fat	8.1g
Protein	4.8g

Estimated Budget: $7.00

Ingredients:

- 7 ounces of jalapeño peppers (cleaned, halved, & seeded)
- ½ pound of soft cream cheese
- 8 ounces of shredded cheddar
- 1 teaspoon of bacon bits (you can remove this for a vegetarian option)
- ⅗ cup of all-purpose flour
- ⅗ cup of milk
- ⅗ cup of breadcrumbs
- About 5 cups of oil for frying (or less if you do this in batches)

Instructions:

1. Mix together the cream cheese, cheddar, and bacon bits in a medium-sized bowl.
2. Spread the halved jalapeños on a plate/tray, hollow side facing up, and evenly spoon the cheese and bacon mixture into the peppers.
3. In two small separate bowls, pour the milk in one and the flour in the other. Dip the jalapeños in the milk and then coat them in flour, then place them back on your plate/tray to sit for about 10 minutes.
4. While the jalapeños are drying, get a medium-sized deep-set dish/bowl and pour the breadcrumbs into it. In this time, you can also set

a skillet on the stove, pour the oil in, and bring the heat to medium high.

5. Once the peppers have dried a bit, dip them back into the milk and then coat them in the breadcrumbs.

6. Once the oil is ready to fry (you can place your hand a few inches above the pan to feel the heat), place the poppers into the pan. Make sure to only fry a few at a time so that they don't stick together. Fry the poppers for about 3 minutes each, until they are golden brown and crispy.

7. Place a paper towel over a bowl. Using a fork or a slotted spoon, scoop the poppers out and place them over the paper towel to drain the excess oil out.

8. Serve with a dipping sauce of choice.

SPINACH TARTE SOLEIL

Bringing the theme back to yet another crisp pastry treat, another amazing recipe is the Spinach Tarte Soleil. This light, tart, French-inspired appetizer is a "pull-apart puff pastry" and is a fantastic, interactive dish that's guaranteed to keep the guests entertained!

Difficulty Level: 7
Preparation Time: 35 minutes
Cooking Time: 35 minutes
Total Time: 70 minutes

Nutritional Info Per Serving Servings: 6-8	
Calories	444
Carbohydrates	36.3g
Fat	29.7g
Protein	10.3g

Estimated Budget: $7.00

Ingredients:

- 17-ounce puff pastry (2 sheets), defrosted

- 20 ounces of frozen spinach (2 10-ounce frozen packs), leave to thaw in the refrigerator one day prior to cooking.
- 2 ½ ounces of Greek Feta, crumbled
- 2 scallions
- 2 tbsps of dill
- 2 cloves of garlic
- 1 lemon
- Salt & pepper to taste
- All-purpose flour (for coating your workspace & rolling)
- 1 large egg
- Hot sauce/dipping sauce (optional addition)

Instructions:

1. On a baking tray lined with parchment paper, place the puff pastry and let it rest for about 10 minutes before unfolding and flattening the pastry out (try to flip them over after about 5 minutes so that they settle nicely).
2. In the interim, place a sieve over a bowl and pour the spinach into it so that the extra juices are drained out. Set aside.
3. Finely chop the 2 scallions and dill, then add both into a bowl. Mix the crumbled Feta into the bowl, and then grate your 2 cloves of garlic and ½ a lemon's worth of lemon zest into the bowl. Sprinkle salt and black pepper into the bowl, to taste. Mix the ingredients together.

4. Using a paper towel, gently press out the excess moisture in the spinach (you will want to get the spinach as dry as possible so that the pastry isn't soggy). Then finely chop the spinach and combine it into the bowl with the scallions. Stir well.

5. By now, the pastry should be ready. Unfold the pastries and find a large circular object (like a plate) that's about 12" in diameter. Layer parchment paper over the object and then place one of the pastry sheets on top of it. Lightly sprinkle some flour on the pastry and roll it out, rotating 90° at a time (so that all of the sides are equally rolled out). You should aim to roll the pastry sheet until it's about 1" larger than your round object.

6. Place the round object on top of the pastry sheet, and using a knife, carve around the round object so that you have a clean circular pastry shape. Repeat the process with the second pastry sheet.

7. Now it's time to egg wash the pastry. Crack the egg in a small bowl and beat it with a fork. With the pastry on a baking sheet, lightly egg wash the circumference of it. Note: Leave some egg wash remainder for later.

8. Pour your spinach mixture into the center of the pastry circle (make sure to leave about a ½" border around the pastry). Place the second circular pastry on top of the other and gently

press around the edges of the pastries to seal it nice and shut (similar to making a pie).

9. Using a smaller round object (like a cup), find the center of your pastry circle and make a smaller, circular indent using the cup/object.

10. Transfer the pastry (on its parchment paper) onto the baking sheet.

11. Starting from the edge of the inner circular indent, cut the pastry into quarters (so that the pastry is now in four wedges that are all connected at the inner circle). Halve each quadrant again and repeat the process until you have 16 equal spokes.

12. Starting from the inner part of the circle, gently twist one spoke at a time. Pop in the freezer for 10-15 minutes.

13. Preheat the oven to 400°F in the interim.

14. Remove the pastry from the freezer and lightly brush over the pastry with the remaining egg wash. Sprinkle salt and pepper to taste, then pop in the oven for 30-35 minutes, until golden brown.

15. Serve with a dipping sauce of choice.

DARK SOY SAUCE CHICKEN WINGS

Needless to say, chicken wings (especially the ones with the best sticky sauces) are a win for any occasion. Chicken wings have always been a favorite crowd pleaser and an amazing comfort food, and it all comes down to one key factor—the flavorful sauce that the wings are doused in! This wing recipe ensures that it's all about the flavor, the spices, and the experience. Inspired by Taiwanese flavors, here's a gourmet recipe that's tantalizingly tart and delicious.

Note: Consider making the spice mix ahead of time as it will allow the spices to mix well together. Try to make it about a week prior, but if you're short on time, you can make it on the day.

Difficulty Level: 8
Preparation Time: 30 minutes (excluding time for the spice mix)
Cooking Time: 40 minutes
Total Time: 70 minutes

Nutritional Info Per Serving Servings: 16 wings	
Calories	373

Carbohydrates	5.5g
Fat	13.9g
Protein	53.7g

Estimated Budget: $12.00-$15.00

Ingredients:

Spice Mix:

- 2 ½ cinnamon sticks (each stick about 4" in length)
- 20-star anise
- 1 ½ whole garlic cloves
- 3 ¼ tbsp of Sichuan pepper
- 2 ½ tsp of fennel seeds
- 1 tsp of black pepper
- 1 tsp of white pepper
- ¼ tsp of cumin powder
- 20 slices of dried ginger (optional)

Chicken Wings:

- 2 ½ lb of chicken wings (about 20 pieces)
- ½ cup of dark soy sauce
- 3 tbsps of vegetable oil
- 2 pieces of ginger (about 3" each), thinly sliced
- 1 shallot, thinly sliced
- 3 scallions, halved & roots removed

- 5 smashed garlic cloves
- 1 Fresno chile
- ¼ cup of cane/raw sugar
- 3 star anise
- 1 cinnamon stick (about 4" in length)
- ¼ tsp Sichuan pepper
- ¼ tsp white pepper
- ⅓ cup of soy sauce
- ¼ cup of unseasoned rice wine (if seasoned, adjust your spices & seasoning accordingly)
- 2 pieces of dried licorice root (optional)
- 2 tbsps of sesame seeds (optional)
- ½ tsp of lemon juice
- ½ scallion, finely chopped (for garnish)

Instructions:

1. For the spice mix: in a small pan over medium heat, toss in your cinnamon sticks, star anise, cloves, Sichuan peppers, licorice root, black and white pepper, and dried ginger (if you're using this ingredient). Toast for about 3 minutes, stirring gently with (preferably) a wooden spoon, until the aromas of the spices awaken. Once the mix has cooled, place in a coffee grinder, spice mill, or blender (whichever you have is fine), and grind until fine.

2. To prepare the chicken wings: in a medium-sized bowl, combine half of the sliced ginger, ¼ cup of soy sauce, and 1 tsp of the spice mix and stir until

well mixed. Coat the chicken wings in the mixture, cover, and set aside to marinate for 1-8 hours.

3. Once the chicken wings have marinated, drizzle oil into a deep-set pan and bring to a medium-high heat.

4. Add in the shallot, garlic, scallions, chile, and the remainder of the ginger into the pan and cook for about 2 minutes, stirring regularly to infuse the flavors.

5. Add the sugar, star anise, cinnamon sticks, white pepper, Sichuan pepper, licorice root (if you're using this), and the 1 tsp remainder of the spice mix into the pan and stir.

6. Next, reduce the heat to a medium low, and pour in the soy sauce, dark soy sauce, and ¼ cup of water.

7. Individually, add the chicken wings into the pan and pour the leftover marinade in, as well as the wine. Stir the wings to coat well in the sauce and bring to a simmer. Cover the pan and allow it to cook for 15 minutes. Stir the chicken and check the wings for a darkened brown color, then cover and leave for another 15 minutes.

8. Use a slotted spoon to remove the wings from the pan and place in a dish/plate.

9. Strain the remaining sauce from the pan into a separate, small bowl. Discard the solid ingredients. Place the contents within the small bowl back into the pan and cook over medium-

high heat for an additional 10 minutes (it should turn into a thick sauce).

10. Place the chicken wings back into the pan and coat them well in the sauce.

11. Plate the wings and sprinkle sesame seeds over the top (if using). Garnish with the ½ chopped scallion and a sprinkle of lemon juice.

Chapter Two

VEGETARIAN

In this chapter, our aim was to incorporate a few things—fast-food inspired recipes, healthy recipes, recipes that mimic meat options, and recipes that are interesting, challenging, and unique in taste!

So, for the first recipe that we decided to tackle, we considered what the most famous fast-food meal was—a burger. And in considering this, it's unfortunate to note how many of our main franchise fast-food outlets have extremely few vegetarian options. There are usually french fries, and if you're lucky, a soya/vegetarian burger option. It tends to get dreary and unexciting, not only for the ones who have been vegetarian their whole lives, but also for the ones who are new to the diet—it's tough, to say the least. Saying that, we thought we'd bring some zest for life back into how exciting and expansive the vegetarian diet can actually be! We've added a recipe for a delicious, crispy vegetarian burger patty that's quick to make and high in protein. In doing so, hopefully this sparks your interest in experimenting with other, similar versions of this burger patty recipe to see how many great options there are out there.

The aim in this chapter is to show you how vastly expansive and exciting the vegetarian diet can be (the power of good, fresh produce mixed with the right combination of spices, can be so powerful that you won't even notice that the dish is meat free).

A few other recipes that were included in this chapter are butternut torte, paneer masala (an Indian cuisine that makes use of a cheese similar to halloumi), cauliflower tacos, and lastly, vegetarian sloppy joes–because we can!

Our vegetarian inspired fast foods aren't only aimed at the regular ol' hamburgers (which we still covered, because inclusivity). We also tackle the more in detail fast-food recipes. Now you can enjoy a sloppy joe with your friends at a sports match, or even at a get-together BBQ at a friend's place. Add in a challenge while you're at it and see if your friends can even tell the difference between the meaty sloppy joe and the vegetarian one! Not to mention, the vegetarian burger patty and sloppy joe are much, much healthier than the meaty ones. They provide a lean source of protein and nutrition, to keep you energized through the day.

With these few recipes from around the world (and your favorite restaurants and take-out spots), you're sorted for any occasion!

CHICKPEA & SPINACH PATTIES

When it comes to vegetarian burgers, sadly there aren't as many options in restaurants in comparison to the numerous possibilities that vegetables can offer. Vegetarian burger patties are normally only offered (in restaurants) as ground soya, but there's such an expansive range of vegetable patties that one can make at home. Not to mention, it's much more healthy, nutritious, and delicious! One of the tastier patty options is this chickpea and spinach patty–it's flavorful in spice and offers a fantastic boost of protein and iron.

Difficulty Level: 3
Preparation Time: 10 minutes
Cooking Time: 10 minutes
Total Time: 20 minutes

Nutritional Info Per Serving	
Servings: 4 patties. 1 patty per serving	
Calories	180
Carbohydrates	21g
Fat	7.5g
Protein	8g

Estimated Budget: $6.00

Ingredients:

- ¼ cup of crumbled Feta
- 1 clove of garlic (alternatively, you can use ½ tsp of garlic paste)
- 1 jalapeño, seeded
- ¼ cup of sesame seeds
- ½ chopped chili (optional)
- ½ cup of spinach
- 2 scallions, quartered
- ½ cup of cooked quinoa
- 1 can of chickpeas, rinsed
- 1 tbsp of olive oil
- Salt & pepper to taste
- A sprinkle of mixed herbs
- Sweet soy sauce for drizzling over

Instructions:

1. Preheat the oven to 475°F.
2. Combine the Feta, garlic, jalapeño, salt, pepper, chili (if you're using), and herbs in a food processor and mix until almost smooth–it should resemble a nut butter texture.
3. Add the spinach, chickpeas, sesame seeds, quinoa, and scallions into the processor and pulse a few more times to combine. It should now be a bit thicker in texture.

4. Prepare a baking tray by drizzling the oil over the top so as to lightly coat the surface. Spoon out the mixture by dolloping small, golf-ball sized shapes (or bigger, if you'd like bigger patties) onto the tray—leaving enough space between each ball. Flatten the balls by pressing the spoon on them, or using your hands, so that it creates patty shapes.

5. Pop into the oven for about 8 minutes, until golden brown, and then turn the patties over and leave to roast for another 8 minutes.

6. Lightly drizzle the soy sauce over the patties and serve with a salad, or in a burger bun of your choice.

CAULIFLOWER TACOS

A perfectly balanced recipe is something that can both satisfy your cravings, as well as be filled with nutritional benefits. This cauliflower taco recipe is a winner at that! If you're in the mood for some Mexican food, definitely give this recipe a go. The zesty sauce complements the crunchy cauliflower, and they are all tied together with a soft tortilla; it's the perfect option for a summer lunch.

Difficulty Level: 5
Preparation Time: 30 minutes
Cooking Time: 30 minutes
Total Time: 1 hour

Nutritional Info Per Serving	
Calories	233
Carbohydrates	31.5g
Fat	7.2g
Protein	9.6g

Estimated Budget: $10.00

Ingredients:

Crumbed Cauliflower:

- 1 medium cauliflower head (cleaned and separated into florets)
- ½ cup of panko breadcrumbs
- ½ cup of cornmeal
- 1 tsp of cumin
- 1 tsp of paprika
- ¼ tsp of turmeric
- ½ tsp of salt
- 1 tbsp of coconut oil
- 1 tbsp of peanut butter
- 1 tbsp of maple syrup
- 2 tbsps of soy sauce
- ½ tsp of hot sauce

Tacos:

- 8 soft corn tortillas
- Crumbed cauliflower pieces
- 1 can of refried beans (15 ounces)
- ½ tsp of cumin
- 2 cups of shredded red cabbage
- 2 limes
- 3 tbsps of Spicy Chipotle Sauce (you can substitute this for something milder, such as mayo)

Instructions:

Prepare the crumbed cauliflower first:

1. Start by preheating the oven to 400°F, then wash and separate the cauliflower head into medium-large florets.
2. Combine the panko breadcrumbs, cornmeal, cumin, smoked paprika, garlic powder, turmeric, and salt in a small bowl.
3. Place a small pan over medium heat and pour the coconut oil, peanut butter, maple syrup, soy sauce, and hot sauce into the pan. Whisk slowly to combine the mixture while it melts. The mixture should turn dark brown in color. After about 2 minutes, remove the sauce from the heat.
4. On a baking tray lined with parchment paper, lay out the cauliflower florets and then evenly pour the sauce mixture over the florets, coating well.
5. Individually, take each floret and dip it into the bowl of the crumbed mixture. Dip the floret back into the sauce mixture, then dip the floret once more in the crumbed mix, and finally place it back onto the tray. Repeat this process with each floret.
6. Place the cauliflower florets into the oven and bake for 30 minutes, turning them over halfway through. You can enjoy these as a snack or incorporate them into a meal.

Now for the fun part—assembling the tacos!

1. Pour the contents of the refried beans into a bowl and mix in a pinch of salt.
2. Shred your cabbage and place into a separate bowl. Squeeze in a desirable amount of lime juice and mix well.
3. Warm the tortillas by placing them on a medium-heat pan for 30 seconds each (alternatively, you can pop them in the microwave to save on time).
4. Plate the tortilla. Add a handful of shredded cabbage, refried beans, and shredded cheese into the center of the tortilla. Place two cauliflower florets in each tortilla and drizzle your sauce of choice over the top. Enjoy this light, zesty, and crunchy wrap!

BUTTERNUT TORTE

A torte is essentially a fancy way of saying the meal has layers. Similar to a lasagna-style dish, this recipe makes use of butternut and other wholesome roast vegetables. The best part about this recipe is that there's no bread, pasta, or rice incorporated into the dish. You'll be getting your carbohydrates from vegetables such as the butternut and potatoes. It offers a heartier, warmer meal which is light and perfect for a wintery dinner! It will also go well with a meat dish if you're having a big get-together; therefore, there'll be something tasty on the table for everyone to dig into.

Difficulty Level: 4
Preparation Time: 15 minutes
Cooking Time: 45 minutes
Total Time: 1 hour

Nutritional Info Per Serving Servings: 4	
Calories	310
Carbohydrates	27.3g
Fat	16.6g
Protein	16.2g

Estimated Budget: $9.00

Ingredients:

- 1/2 small butternut squash (1 lb)
- 1 medium potato
- 1 tbsp olive oil
- 1 red onion
- 1 small bunch kale
- 6 oz provolone cheese
- 1 tomato
- 1 oz parmesan
- A pinch of rosemary & thyme
- A pinch of paprika
- Salt & pepper to taste
- 2 tbsps of fresh cream (for garnishing)
- A pinch of coconut shavings (for garnishing)

Instructions:

1. Preheat your oven to 425°F.
2. Wash and slice your butternut squash, tomato, and potato into thin slices. Cut the onion into thin slices and separate the rings. Set the contents aside.
3. Take a springform pan (if you don't have this, you can use a small casserole dish), and lightly coat the surface of the pan with oil.
4. Layer some of the butternut squash slices in a circular form on the base of the pan. Layer a few

onion rings, then half of the kale. Drizzle a little more oil over the kale and season with salt, pepper, and paprika.

5. Layer the potato slices on top of the kale, then layer on the provolone cheese.

6. Use the remainder of the kale on the next layer, and repeat by drizzling oil and seasoning with salt and pepper. Next, add more onion rings, tomato slices, and provolone.

7. Lastly, add the top layer of butternut squash on the top. Sprinkle the top layer with parmesan cheese, rosemary, and thyme.

8. Cover the dish with foil and pop into the oven for 20 minutes.

9. Remove the foil and set the oven to broil, and pop the dish back into the oven for another 10 minutes, until the top turns a golden brown in color.

10. Serve warm.

SLOPPY JOE

Nothing screams juicy, saucy comfort food like a sloppy joe! Not only is it easy to whip up, it's so filling and satisfying! This recipe is the perfect vegetarian substitute, incorporating the sauces, spices, and vegetables in a warm, soft bun. Perfect for a Sunday barbeque or catching up with some friends to watch the big game, this sloppy joe recipe will perfectly complement the atmosphere. This recipe asks for quite a few ingredients, but it's easy and quick to whip up.

*An important note for this recipe is that sloppy joes traditionally contain Worcestershire sauce (which might contain anchovies/fish sauce in its mixture). We have incorporated a vegan Worcestershire recipe below for your consideration, if you have a stricter diet.

Difficulty Level: 4
Preparation Time: 30 minutes
Cooking Time: 15 minutes
Total Time: 45 minutes

Nutritional Info Per Serving Servings: 6 Sloppy Joes	
Calories	335
Carbohydrates	43g

Fat	10.2g
Protein	19.6g

Estimated Budget: $5.00-$7.00

Ingredients:

Vegan Worcestershire Sauce:

- 1 cup of apple cider vinegar
- ⅓ cup of soy sauce
- 1 tsp Dijon mustard
- 3 tbsp of brown sugar
- ½ tsp of allspice (nutmeg, cinnamon and cloves)
- ½ tsp of garlic powder
- ½ tsp of onion powder
- ⅛ tsp of black pepper

Sloppy Joe:

- ¼ cup of vegetable oil
- ½ cup of minced onion
- ¼ tsp of ground cumin
- ¼ tsp of turmeric
- ½ tsp ground coriander
- ½ tsp of dried thyme
- ½ tsp of oregano
- ½ tsp of paprika
- ½ tsp of chili flakes (optional)

- 16 ounces of tempeh
- ½ cup of minced bell pepper
- 1 tbsp of garlic paste
- ¼ cup of tomato sauce
- 1 ½ tbsp of honey
- 1 tbsp of Vegan Worcestershire Sauce
- Hot sauce (optional)
- 6 burger buns
- Salt & pepper to taste

Instructions:

For the Vegan Worcestershire Sauce:

1. In a small pot over medium heat, combine all of the sauce ingredients into the pan and stir well. Leave to simmer and cover the pot. Cook for about 5 minutes and then leave to cool down.

For the Sloppy Joe:

1. Fry the onion in a bit of oil over a medium heat, until the onion turns a golden brown. Pour in the spices: cumin, turmeric, coriander, thyme, oregano, chili flakes (if you're using), and paprika, then crumble in the tempeh. Mix with a wooden spoon, preferably.
2. Once the aromas of the spices have awakened, add in the green pepper and garlic, stirring for another 2 minutes until softened.

3. Finally, mix in the tomato sauce, honey, and Vegan Worcestershire Sauce. Stir well, cover the pan, and leave to simmer for 10-15 minutes.
4. While the mix is simmering, prepare your buns by cutting the buns in half. Once the mix has cooked well and is aromatic, spoon the mix into the buns and enjoy!

PANEER MASALA

This delightfully creamy dish roots itself in India. It's famous for its glorious balance of spice-to-cream ratio, perfect for the colder, winter nights, or if you're simply looking for a homely meal to enjoy! "Paneer" is a type of cheese, also rooting itself in India. It's similar to halloumi cheese but doesn't melt when heated. Paneer Masala might be a tough challenge to take on at first, but its creamy deliciousness is definitely worth it. Once you get the basic understanding of how a curry is made, with practice, this recipe is a piece of cake!

Note: This recipe makes use of cashews. You can remove this ingredient if you're allergic. It's optional for this recipe.

Difficulty Level: 6
Preparation Time: 10 minutes
Cooking Time: 20 minutes
Total Time: 30 minutes

Nutritional Info Per Serving Servings: 4	
Calories	166
Carbohydrates	17.5g
Fat	9.4g

Protein	4.8g

Estimated Budget: $12.00 (with cashew nuts incl.)

Ingredients:

Curry gravy:

- 1 tbsp of vegetable oil
- 2 elaichis (green cardamoms)
- 1 cup of diced onions
- 1 ½ cups of diced tomato
- ¾ tsp of chili powder
- ¾ tsp of garam masala
- 1 tsp of coriander
- ½ tsp of turmeric
- ¾ tsp of sugar
- Salt to taste
- 12 cashews (optional)

Paneer Masala:

- 1 ½ tbsps of butter
- 1 bay leaf
- 1" cinnamon stick
- 2 cloves
- 2 elaichis (green cardamoms)
- 1 ½ tsps of garlic & ginger paste
- ¼ tsp chili powder
- 7 ounces of paneer

- ¾ tsp of dried fenugreek
- 3 tbsps of cream
- 2 tbsps of coriander leaves (for garnishing)

Instructions:

1. In a small pan over medium heat, add in your 1 tbsp of oil, 2 elaichis, garam masala, coriander powder, ¾ tsp chili powder, and the onion. Fry for about 2 minutes until the onion has softened and is fragrant.

2. Pour in the diced tomato, cashew nuts, sugar, and salt, then cook for another 3 minutes, stirring regularly to combine the flavors. Cover the pan and leave to simmer for another 2 minutes.

3. Stir once more to mix the contents well and then set aside to cool.

4. Once almost cooled down, pour the contents into a blender with 1 cup of water and blend until the mixture is a smooth paste. Set the tomato purée aside.

5. Now to prepare the paneer. In a medium, deep-set pan (or pot), melt the butter over medium-high heat, then mix in the cinnamon stick, cloves, 2 remaining elaichis, bay leaf, and the ginger and garlic paste. Reduce the heat to a medium low and stir to integrate all of the flavors. Fry for about 1-2 minutes until the aromas awaken–be careful not to burn the ginger paste. It's important to stir it regularly.

6. After about 2 minutes of frying, add in the tomato purée mix that you have just made and ¼ tsp of chili powder. Stir well to mix the flavors together. You might have to add ¼ cup of water at a time into the pan, if the tomato purée is still too thick. Mix well and add the water by discretion to get a smooth consistency. Lower the heat to a low, and leave to cook for about 10 minutes, stirring regularly, until the sauce thickens.

7. After 10 minutes, stir in the paneer and fenugreek and leave for about 1 minute before pouring the cream in. Stir once more, cover, and leave to simmer for 2-3 minutes.

8. Stir one last time before plating. Drizzle a little cream over the top of each serving and garnish with coriander. Best served with rice.

Chapter Three

FAST FOOD

We've finally reached the precise point of *Copycat Recipes* where the title firmly holds true to its own name: we would kindly like to introduce you to… copycat fast-food recipes!

This is the part of the cookbook where it all goes down! All the fast-food cravings that you were eagerly awaiting—it all happens right here! We've narrowed our list down to the top five take-out joints that are the epitome of what you would think of when you hear the word "fast food."

Now, not to fret, we have incorporated other fast-food inspired recipes throughout the rest of the book where they work well into other chapter topics. This chapter is dedicated specifically to, again, the epitome of fast-food outlets.

In the running we have strong and steady Colonel Sanders himself. There's never *not* an occasion where a large bucket of KFC fried chicken can't help soothe the situation… it's soul food for a reason! So, of course, we had to incorporate a KFC chicken inspired recipe to soothe all of our isolation blues. Next up in the running, we have the one and only Wendy's famous chili. This delightfully spicy chili is unfathomably, mouth-wateringly delicious. It screams comfort food. So, naturally, adding a homemade chili recipe into the mix only seemed fair.

What's a perfect dish to go with chili, you may ask? Sonic's deep-fried corn dogs! These are delicious, fit every occasion, and seem an oddly festive meal to make at home, but why not? That's the beauty of these homemade, copycat fast-food recipes.

Next up, we have two of America's most famous pizza styles: Chicago deep-dish pizza and the one, the only, pizza pretzels! Chicago deep-dish pizza is perfect if you want to prepare a few days' worth of dinner/lunch as it's quite a lengthy (but totally worth it) process. Whereas the pizza pretzels are much faster to make and are a perfect way to reminisce back on the Macy's Thanksgiving Day Parade, all year round!

PIZZA PRETZELS

Care for a crusted pizza exterior that oozes with melted cheese and tomato paste with each bite? Sounds like the perfect combination! This glorious innovation mixes two of our favorite fast-food dishes: pizza and pretzels. It's an extremely easy (and fun) recipe to make, and it's perfect for any occasion, whether it's a lunchtime snack, a quick bite to take along on a picnic, or a simple weekend get-together with a few friends; this delicious meal should take a quick 40 minutes (with baking) and is a great addition to any occasion! The best part? It only requires a few staple ingredients.

Note: this recipe makes use of store-bought pizza dough. If you'd like to make your own homemade dough, we've also included it in this recipe.

Difficulty Level: 5

Preparation Time: 20 minutes (excluding making homemade pizza dough)

Cooking Time: 20 minutes (excluding making homemade pizza dough)

Total Time: 40 minutes

Nutritional Info Per Serving **Servings:** 3 pretzels	
Calories	935
Carbohydrates	63.8g
Fat	63.5g
Protein	28.1g

Estimated Budget: $12.00

Ingredients:

- 1 14oz tube of store-bought pizza dough (refer to recipe below to make homemade dough)
- 4 cups of shredded mozzarella cheese
- ¼ cup of crumbled Feta cheese
- 15 slices of pepperoni
- ¾ can of tomato paste
- Mixed herbs, to taste
- Cooking spray

For homemade pizza dough:

- 0.25-ounce pack of dry yeast
- 1 tsp of white sugar
- 1 cup of warm water
- 2 tbsps of olive oil
- 1 tsp of salt

- 2 ½ cups of all-purpose flour

Instructions:

For the homemade pizza dough:

1. Dissolve the yeast and sugar in a bowl with warm water, stirring regularly. This should take about 5-8 minutes. Then mix in the oil, salt, and flour and slowly beat the mixture. Let it rest for another 5 minutes. Then, using your fists, gently knead into the dough so that it loses all of the air bubbles, and the ingredients combine well together.
2. Lightly flour a working surface and transfer the dough onto the surface. Roll the dough out, using a rolling pin. Aim to roll the dough into a rectangular shape for this recipe, about 15x9-inches.

For the Pizza Pretzels:

1. Preheat your oven to 425°F.
2. On a lightly floured workspace, unroll the store-bought dough or have your homemade dough ready. Cut the rectangular dough (15x9-inches) into 3 equal strips, lengthwise.
3. Then further roll each strip of dough to about 3" in width and 34" in length. Keep a cup of flour near you as you work, as you may need to add more flour as you go along the process (if the dough becomes too sticky).

4. Evenly spread ½ of the can of tomato paste in the center of each of the strips (it should be a light spread–you don't want the pretzel to be too overwhelming with tomato paste). Reserve the last ¼ cup of the tomato paste for later.

5. Next, sprinkle 1 cup of mozzarella down the center of each strip, then generously sprinkle some mixed herbs in each strip.

6. Fold one side of one of the strips over, connecting it to the other side (creating a round tube-like shape). Repeat this process with the other strips.

7. Prepare a baking sheet by layering it with a sheet of foil and spraying it with cooking spray, then transfer the pizza tubes onto the baking tray.

8. To create the pretzel shape, take one end of one of the pizza tubes and create a circular shape, by having the two edges meet. Next, take both of the edges and twist them once, over each other, and rest on the opposite end of the pretzel shape. Repeat this process with the other pizza tubes.

9. Lastly, brush over the top of the pretzels with the remainder of the tomato paste, then layer on the pepperoni slices and sprinkle the last cup of mozzarella and feta cheese.

10. Pop the pretzels into the oven for about 15 minutes until the pizzas are golden brown. Then set your oven to broil and pop the pretzels back in for 2 more minutes, so that the tops are nice and crusted!

SONIC-STYLE CORN DOGS

Inspired by the American drive-in franchise, Sonic—one of their customers' all-time favorite snacks has got to be their famous corn dogs! Consisting merely of sausage dipped in batter and deep fried, this recipe is guaranteed to be an easy, homemade meal and will comfort all of those fast-food cravings! The secret to this recipe is found in the batter and cornmeal: spice it right, and you've got yourself a winning corn dog.

Difficulty Level: 5
Preparation Time: 10 minutes
Cooking Time: 25 minutes
Total Time: 35 minutes

Nutritional Info Per Serving Servings: 12 (a dozen) corn dogs	
Calories	284
Carbohydrates	18g
Fat	19.2g
Protein	9.9g

Estimated Budget: $8.00

Ingredients:

- 1 cup of all-purpose flour
- ½ cup of yellow cornmeal
- 1 tbsp of sugar
- 3 tsps of baking powder
- ½ tsp of ground mustard (optional, this can also be removed if you're using mustard sauce as a dip)
- ¼ tsp of paprika
- ½ tsp of salt
- ½ tsp of pepper
- 1 egg, beaten
- 1 cup of evaporated milk
- 12 wooden skewers
- 12 hot dogs (vegetarians can substitute this with soya hot dogs/vegetarian hot dogs)
- Oil for frying

Instructions:

1. Pour a generous amount of oil into a deep-set pan or pot for frying, and preheat the oil to about 375°F (medium high).
2. Combine the flour, cornmeal, sugar, baking powder, ground mustard (if using), paprika, salt, and pepper in a bowl and gently whisk together.
3. Slowly pour in the egg and milk while whisking.

4. Pierce a skewer through each hot dog, lengthwise, and insert the hot dog into the batter that you just mixed together.

5. Place a few corn dogs into the oil at a time (to prevent them from sticking together) and turn them over a few times, using tongs/a spoon. Fry for about 2-3 minutes each, until the corn dogs are golden brown.

6. Place a paper towel over a plate/bowl and transfer the fried corn dogs onto the paper towel so that the excess oil is drained. Serve hot and with your desired sauces.

DEEP DISH PIZZA

Deep dish pizza has its roots in the heart of Chicago. In keeping with the pizza theme, it's only fair to pay homage to one of the most popular, unique, and flavorful styles of pizza that there is. Chicago-style deep dish pizza is exactly what its name implies—similar to a pie without its top layer, deep dish pizza oozes with pizza filling and has a thick, puffy crusted base. It's famous for its thick, melted cheese, thus making it one of the most *perfect* types of comfort food. This recipe is a bit more time consuming due to the homemade pizza dough, but the results in taste will definitely make it all worth it at the end!

Note: You will need to allow time for the dough to rise properly, so time management is key here. Aim to make the dough at least an hour prior to the pizza. This recipe also makes two pizzas, so prepare two oven dishes for this recipe; otherwise, you can always freeze the extra dough and sauce for a later use.

Difficulty Level: 8

Preparation Time: 2 hours 30 minutes (for allowing the dough to rise)

Cooking Time: 30 minutes

Total Time: 3 hours

Nutritional Info Per Serving
Servings: 4

Calories	750
Carbohydrates	98.2g
Fat	29.9g
Protein	22.9g

Estimated Budget: $7.00

Ingredients:

For the pizza crust:

- 3 ½ cups of all-purpose flour
- ½ cup of yellow cornmeal
- 1 ¼ tsps of salt
- 1 tbsp of sugar
- 1 packet of yeast
- 1 ¼ cups of warm water
- ½ cup of unsalted, melted butter, divided (if you're using salted butter, remove the salt from the ingredients list)
- 1 tbsp of olive oil

For the sauce:

- 2 tbsps of unsalted butter (again, if you're using salted butter, remove the salt from the ingredients list)
- 1 onion, diced
- ¾ tsp of salt
- 1 tsp of dried oregano
- ½ tsp of chili flakes
- 2 tbsps of garlic paste/minced garlic
- 1 can of crushed tomatoes
- ¼ tsp of sugar
- A pinch of mixed herbs spice

For topping:

- 4 cups of shredded mozzarella
- ½ cup of grated parmesan
- Optional: pepperoni, green peppers, mushroom.

Instructions:

Preparing the pizza crust:

1. In a medium/large bowl, combine the flour, cornmeal, salt, sugar, and yeast. Mix well until the ingredients are well combined (using your hands to mix this will give the best results).
2. Next, add in ¼ of the melted butter and warm water, stirring with a wooden spoon. Mix the dough until it has a soft, supple feel. If it's too

hard, slowly add more water as you mix. If it's too soft/sticky, add in a few more spoons of flour until the texture is right. It should be soft and not sticky.

3. Find an ovenproof dish and drizzle a little olive oil around the edges, then place the dough into the dish.

4. Preheat your oven to 250°F.

5. Cover the dish with foil and place it in the oven for about an hour until the dough has risen (about double its size).

6. When the dough is almost ready, lightly flour a working space. Remove the dough from the oven and place the foil aside (you will be using it again soon). Carefully knead into the dough to further remove any air bubbles and then place the dough on the floured working space.

7. Roll out the dough into a large rectangular shape, about 15x12" in dimension.

8. Spread the last ¼ cup of butter over the dough and then roll the dough up (like a swiss roll) and cut it in half. Roll these two halves into balls and pop them back into the oven dish, cover with foil, and place back into the refrigerator for about an hour, while you prepare the pizza sauce.

Preparing the sauce:

1. In a pan over medium heat, melt the butter and then add in your onion, oregano, chili flakes, and

salt. Stir for about 5 minutes until fragrant and the onion bits have softened.

2. Add the garlic, sugar, a pinch of mixed herbs, and tomatoes into the pan and reduce the heat to medium-low. Allow the contents to simmer for 30 minutes, stirring regularly.

3. Once the pizza dough has turned puffy and light brown (after an hour), remove it from the refrigerator and turn the oven back on, preheating it to 425°F.

Putting the pizza together:

1. Roll the pizza dough balls out over a lightly floured working space. Roll it into about 12-inch circles (or to the shape and dimension of the oven dish that you're using). Aim to make the dough a little bigger than the dish that you're using, as you'll need extra dough around the edges to form the crust.

2. Place the dough into two separate oven dishes (if you only have one dish, then you'll need to make two batches). Use your fingers to press the dough against the edges of the dish, making sure that it's firm.

3. Lightly drizzle olive oil over the crusted edge and then fill each pizza with about 2 cups of cheese per pizza, then add in any of your preferred toppings, and then layer on another 1 ¼ cups worth of the pizza sauce. Finally, sprinkle the

mozzarella cheese over the tops and pop the dishes into the oven.

4. Bake for 25-30 minutes and serve warm!

KFC INSPIRED CHICKEN

Soul food stems from southern American cuisine, and their food truly does encompass the name. One of the most favorite soul food dishes is fried chicken, and preparing this meal is much easier than you think! Similar to the corn dog recipe, the secret lies in the spices within the batter. This quick and easy recipe will add an interesting touch to your meal, if you're in the mood for a little crunchy, deep-fried goodness.

Difficulty Level: 4
Preparation Time: 15 minutes
Cooking Time: 15 minutes
Total Time: 30 minutes

Nutritional Info Per Serving Servings: 12 chicken pieces	
Calories	543
Carbohydrates	17g
Fat	33g
Protein	41g

Estimated Budget: $10.00

Ingredients:

- 4 cups of all-purpose flour, divided
- 2 tbsps of garlic powder
- 1 tbsp of paprika
- 3 tsps of pepper, divided
- 2 ½ tsps of poultry seasoning
- 2 eggs
- 1 tsp of salt
- 2 chickens (3 ½ - 4 lb. each), separated into pieces
- Oil for deep-frying

Instructions:

1. Fill a pot/deep-set pan about halfway with oil and bring the temperature to medium high.
2. Mix together 2 cups of flour, garlic powder, paprika, 2 tsps of pepper, and the poultry seasoning in a large bowl.
3. In a separate medium-large bowl, mix together the eggs, 1 ½ cups of water, salt, the remainder of the flour, and remainder of the pepper. Beat the eggs and combine all of the contents together.
4. Coat each piece of chicken with the egg mixture first, then with the flour mixture. Coat the chicken pieces well so that they're covered all-round.
5. Working with a few pieces at a time, deep fry the chicken for about 7-8 minutes and then turn the

chicken pieces over, frying for another 7-8 minutes.

6. Lay a paper towel over a plate, next to the stove. Once the chicken pieces are cooked and golden brown, remove them and place them on the paper towel to drain the excess oil.

WENDY'S CHILI

A wintery evening simply beckons for this hearty, spicy chili recipe! Although it may be a bit of a time-consuming process, the amount of flavor and aroma that homemade chili offers is immeasurable. It's the greatest form of self-love if you're looking for something to cheer you up or simply warm you up on a wintery evening! This recipe yields about 10 servings worth of chili, so this is perfect for a dinner get-together, or if you'd like to meal prep for your week ahead!

Note: You will need a slow cooker/pressure cooker for this recipe.

Difficulty Level: 3
Preparation Time: 10 minutes
Cooking Time: 8-10 hours (on the slow cooker)
Total Time: 8-10 hours

Nutritional Info Per Serving Servings: 10	
Calories	257
Carbohydrates	12.9g
Fat	8g
Protein	32.5g

Estimated Budget: $15.00

Ingredients:

- 2 pounds of ground beef (if you're vegetarian, you can substitute this with ground soya)
- 2 cans of kidney beans, rinsed & drained
- 2 onions, diced & divided
- 1 can of diced tomato
- 1 diced green pepper
- 1 tbsp of garlic paste, divided
- 2 tbsps of chili powder
- ¼ tsp of cinnamon
- ½ tsp of mixed herb spice
- Salt & pepper to taste (preferably about 1 tsp each)
- ¼ cup of chopped scallion
- ½ cup shredded cheddar cheese
- 2 tbsps of soy sauce per serving (for drizzling)

Instructions:

1. Pour the ground beef into a pan with a drizzle of oil, half of the diced onion, and half of the garlic paste. Fry the beef until it's browned, stirring regularly to incorporate the flavors and aromas of the onion and garlic. Fry for about 10 minutes.
2. Place the contents from the pan into your slow cooker, along with the kidney beans, tomatoes, green pepper, remainder of the onion, remainder

of the garlic paste, chili powder, cinnamon, mixed herbs, salt, and pepper. Cover the slow cooker and leave on a low setting for 8-10 hours.

3. When serving, sprinkle with cheese and a bit of chopped scallions. Top off the serving with a drizzle of soy sauce and enjoy it warm!

Chapter Four

ITALIAN

After all of that fast food, it's time to see some homely, wholesome meals, and what better place to visit, than Italy?

Famous for the glorious combination of tomato pastes, spices, cheeses, and doughy goodness, Italy has blessed many of our taste buds and stomachs with their foolproof, classic recipes. Their pastas, sauces, and pizzas are forever promising and prominent with the tangy tomato flavors, spicy aromas, and mouth-wateringly, tantalizing overflow of cheese!

In this chapter, we plan to pay homage to the land of our favorite dishes by exploring five key dishes that Italy has successfully gotten right, time and time again. Their recipes are so pure and so classic, that it's worked for them (and for us) for decades upon centuries, without needing to change. And thus, it only seems right to incorporate a few dishes, to bring these meals into our homes.

A few of the classics that we chose to cover include calzones–a favorite, especially in the US. These delights are easy to make, manageable to consume, and absolutely delicious and cheesy! The recipe that we tackle is a quick and easy (and cheesy) one that you can effortlessly whip up if you're in need of a quick and tasty bite. We pay tribute to the one and only spaghetti and meatballs recipe, by incorporating this into the chapter also (it feels incomplete without it, to be fair). This recipe will yield quite a few servings, so you can either make it for a get-together, a family dinner, or prepare it for a few nights' worth of dinner—either way, it's extremely cost effective *and* delicious! If you're looking for a more versatile dish, we've included a parmesan chicken recipe that you can enjoy as is or incorporate into many other dishes throughout the week. Also, there's a healthy antipasto salad recipe that can also work well with any of the above-mentioned recipes or on its own. It's an extremely healthy and light meal, if you're looking for a tangy and zesty salad option. Lastly, there's the primavera salad. We've given a little, adorable introduction to the history behind this pizza which will help you understand the dish a little better. With knowing a meal's history, it adds so much more texture to the dish and a more emotional and atmospheric manner. You'll start to understand the reasoning behind certain ingredients and the stories to how these dishes came about, and why they've been such classic and traditional dishes for all these years. It's quite inspiring and uplifting to understand the stories and passion that went into the cuisine. In that way, you appreciate it so much more!

So, how did Italian food become such a lovable cuisine, worldwide? A lot of it has to do with the fact that it's affordable, yields many servings for the money's worth, and also extremely flavorful! Making use of key ingredients such as tomato bases for the sauce, a carbohydrate (such as pasta/pizza to fill you up), and cheese, which adds that extra layer of rich, creamy texture to the dish, provides an overall fulfilling and well-balanced meal!

So, when diving into the Italian recipes, keep in mind that this key trio of ingredients and the way they complement each other, is what you should aim for. To assist in connecting these ingredients, you have vegetables and herbs and spices, and sometimes a meat can accompany this. Use these ingredients and spices wisely while working to create that well-balanced, complementary trio of tomato, carbohydrates, and cheese.

Now that you've got an understanding of the dishes and how the ingredients work with one another, let's start cooking!

PARMESAN CHICKEN

If you're craving a zesty, cheesy chicken meal yet looking for something simple and classic, then this recipe is for you! It's definitely one of those meals that can be enjoyed on its own, or incorporated into bigger meals–either way, it's delicious and quick to make! Traditionally known as "Chicken Parmigiana" in Italy, it's a glorious combination of homemade crumbed, chicken breasts served in a tomato marinara and cheese. It's perfect for a weekday dinner option and can be incorporated into lunches for the following days! It's zesty, cheesy and meaty–it's all things tasty!

Difficulty Level: 7
Preparation Time: 15 minutes
Cooking Time: 1 hour
Total Time: 1 hour 15 minutes

Nutritional Info Per Serving Servings: 6	
Calories	406
Carbohydrates	39.7g
Fat	10g
Protein	37.4g

Estimated Budget: $7.00

Ingredients:

To prepare the chicken:

- 1 ½ pounds of boneless chicken breasts (about 4 breast pieces)
- 1 ½ cups of panko breadcrumbs
- ½ tsp of garlic powder
- ¼ cup of grated parmesan
- 1 cup of shredded mozzarella
- 2 eggs, beaten
- ½ cup of all-purpose flour
- Salt & pepper to taste
- Oil for frying

To prepare the marinara sauce:

- 2 tbsps of olive oil
- ½ small onion, diced
- 1 can of crushed tomatoes
- 2 tbsps of garlic paste (or 4 cloves of fresh garlic, minced)
- ¼ cup of water
- Salt & pepper to taste
- 1 tsp of chili flakes
- 2 tbsps of parsley for garnishing
- 1 tbsp of grated parmesan for garnishing

Instructions:

1. Preheat your oven to 400°F.
2. Take out 3 medium (preferably) sized bowls and another bowl/plate for your chicken. Fill this first bowl with the panko breadcrumbs, garlic powder, and parmesan cheese. Mix the contents together. In the second bowl, pour your beaten eggs and add 1 tbsp of water. Mix the contents once more. Fill the third bowl with flour.
3. Thoroughly wash your chicken breasts and place them into the last bowl/plate and pat them dry with a paper towel. Season the chicken generously with salt and pepper to your taste.
4. Individually dip each piece of chicken into the flour, then into the egg mixture, and lastly dip it into the breadcrumb mix, then place it back on its tray/plate.
5. Coat the surface of a pan with oil and place over medium-high heat. Once the oil has heated, place the breaded chicken into the pan and fry for 5-7 minutes until golden brown, turning the chicken over halfway through. Place the breast pieces on a paper towel to drain the excess oil.
6. While the chicken is frying, make the marinara sauce. Place a medium pot over medium-high heat and drizzle in 2 tbsps of oil. Pour in your diced onion and garlic and cook for 4 minutes, stirring slowly with a wooden spoon (preferably). Then add in your onions and the ¼ cup of water,

salt, pepper, and chili flakes. Stir well and allow to simmer for 10 minutes. Once the 10 minutes are up, stir once more, then add in the parsley and remove from heat.

7. Lastly, you'll need an oven dish for this step. Pour the marinara into the dish, then add in the crumbed chicken breast pieces. Sprinkle the mozzarella cheese on top of the chicken and pop the dish into the oven for 10-12 minutes.

8. If you'd like the cheese to be extra crispy, set the oven to broil and leave the dish in to broil for another 3 minutes, until the cheese is nice and golden. Make sure to keep an eye on this last step, as you don't want to burn the cheese!

9. Garnish the dish with parsley and serve warm!

CALZONES

Invented in 18th century Naples, calzones are not only delicious but they have also carved a long-lasting mark on our hearts (and in our tummies) throughout the centuries! A calzone is similar to an empanada, only it's made with pizza dough and absolutely *anything* works well as a filling. From spinach, to mushrooms, to meatier options... there is a calzone for every occasion. This recipe makes use of the classic calzone, with tomato base, cheese, and mozzarella, but feel free to make it your own—that's the beauty of calzones!

Difficulty Level: 4
Preparation Time: 10 minutes
Cooking Time: 50 minutes
Total Time: 1 hour

Nutritional Info Per Serving Servings: 4 calzones	
Calories	540
Carbohydrates	46.4g
Fat	32.8g
Protein	14.9g

Estimated Budget: $5.00

Ingredients:

- 0.75 lb of pizza dough (either use store bought, or follow the pizza dough recipe in chapter 2 we made for Pizza Pretzels)
- 1 cup of tomato paste
- 1 cup of ricotta cheese
- ½ cup of sliced pepperoni
- 1 cup of shredded mozzarella
- ½ cup of baby spinach
- Salt to taste
- A pinch of mixed herbs
- All-purpose flour to coat the working surface
- Olive oil for brushing the pastries

Instructions:

1. Preheat the oven to 500°F and lightly grease two baking sheets with cooking spray or oil.
2. Lightly flour a working space and divide the pizza dough into 4 equal quadrants. Roll out one of the dough balls into an 8" circle. Layer a spoonful of tomato paste into the center of the dough, then add a few spinach leaves, a dollop of ricotta, a few slices of pepperoni, and mozzarella. Season with a pinch of salt and a sprinkle of mixed herbs.
3. Fold the dough over (creating a semicircle), then wet the edges of the semicircle with water and gently press down on the edges with your fingers,

to close the filling into the dough. Repeat this process with the other balls of dough.

4. Place the calzones onto the baking trays and brush them with olive oil. Using a knife or scissors, make 3 slits on the top of each of the calzones so that the steam can escape while it's cooking and not get too soggy.

5. Pop the calzones into the oven and bake for 20 minutes. Brush the calzones with oil at the halfway mark. Enjoy it while warm!

SPAGHETTI & MEATBALLS

One of the most famous dishes to come out of Italy has definitely got to be spaghetti and meatballs. It's tantalizingly zesty from the tomato-based sauce, meaty, and filling. Spaghetti and meatballs is an age-old traditional dish that promises a hearty, homely feeling once you taste that first bite. The best part about making this recipe at home is that you yield many more servings for much cheaper!

Difficulty Level: 7
Preparation Time: 20 minutes
Cooking Time: 1 hour
Total Time: 1 hour 20 minutes

Nutritional Info Per Serving Servings: 4	
Calories	738
Carbohydrates	86.7g
Fat	18.4g
Protein	55g

Estimated Budget: $7.00

Ingredients:

- 1 lb of spaghetti
- 1 lb of ground beef (or soya if you're vegetarian)
- ⅓ cup of breadcrumbs
- ¼ cup of grated parmesan
- 1 egg
- 1 tbsp of garlic paste
- ½ tsp of chili flakes
- 2 tbsps of olive oil
- ½ onion, diced
- 1 can of crushed tomatoes
- 1 bay leaf
- Salt & pepper to taste
- ¼ cup of chopped parsley
- Extra parmesan and parsley for garnishing

Instructions:

1. Fill a large pot ¾ full of water and a pinch of salt. Bring the water to a boil and cook the spaghetti until it has softened (about 10 minutes).
2. While the spaghetti is cooking, prepare the meatballs. Using a medium-large bowl, mix the beef with the breadcrumbs, parsley, parmesan, egg, garlic, salt, and chili flakes. Mix well and then, using your hands, form about 16 meatballs.
3. Drain the spaghetti once it's softened, using a colander.

4. Bring another medium-large pot to medium heat and drizzle a little bit of oil in it. Place the meatballs into the pot and cook for about 10 minutes, turning them regularly so that they cook evenly. Transfer the meatballs onto a plate.

5. Pour the diced onion into the pot where the meatballs were, and fry for about 5 minutes until the onions have softened. Next, add in the tomatoes and bay leaf, season with salt and pepper, then reduce the heat to a medium low. Add the meatballs back into the pot with the tomato sauce, cover the pot, and leave to simmer for 10 minutes, stirring regularly. Check for the sauce's consistency. If it's thick, it's ready. If not, leave to simmer for another 5 minutes.

6. Dish the spaghetti onto plates or a serving bowl and top with meatballs and sauce. Sprinkle parmesan on top and garnish with parsley.

Bon Appetit!

PRIMAVERA SKILLET

"Primavera" translated from Italian means "springtime." Whenever you see any form of primavera dish, it should have one prominent factor: vibrant color. Spring is the best time in Italy to harvest the best of their crops; therefore, their meals are vibrant with all the colors of the healthy crops that were harvested. In this recipe, we'll take a look at how to make a delicious, healthy, and wholesome vegetarian pizza that embraces the concept of primavera.

Difficulty Level: 6
Preparation Time: 15 minutes
Cooking Time: 30 minutes
Total Time: 45 minutes

Nutritional Info Per Serving Servings: 4 (2 pizzas)	
Calories	333
Carbohydrates	26.8g
Fat	16.6g
Protein	21.5g

Estimated Budget: $5.00

Ingredients:

- 1 lb of pizza dough (or refer to recipe for Pizza Pretzel for homemade pizza dough recipe)
- ½ head of broccoli, florets separated
- ¼ red onion, sliced thinly
- 2 bell peppers, sliced lengthwise
- 1 cup of cherry tomatoes
- 1 cup of ricotta
- 1 cult of shredded mozzarella
- Salt & pepper to taste
- A pinch of rosemary
- A pinch of thyme
- ¼ cup of crumbled Feta cheese
- Olive oil for drizzling
- Flour to coat a working space

Instructions:

1. Preheat the oven to 400°F.
2. Prepare a baking sheet by drizzling the surface with olive oil. Lay the peppers, onion, broccoli, and tomatoes onto the tray and season with salt and pepper. Toss the contents on the tray and give it a good shake, to mix the vegetables with the oil and seasoning. Sprinkle some rosemary and thyme over some of the vegetables. Place the tray in the oven and let it roast for 18-20 minutes.

3. While the vegetables are roasting, prepare the pizza base. Get another oven-proof skillet/baking tray and drizzle more olive oil on the surface.

4. Lightly flour a working space and roll the dough out onto the workspace. Divide the dough into two equal parts, then using a rolling pin, roll each ball of dough into a circular shape, about 12" in diameter.

5. Place one of the pizza bases onto the baking tray/skillet and brush both of the pizza bases with olive oil.

6. Dollop a spoonful of ricotta in the center of both of the pizza bases and spread it evenly, leaving about 1" around the circumference (as this is now the crust). Then, generously sprinkle mozzarella over the bases.

7. Once the vegetables have roasted, remove them from the oven and raise the oven temperature to 500°F.

8. Evenly spread the vegetables onto the pizzas, then season once more with salt. Finally, crumble Feta cheese over the tops.

9. You can use the second tray (which the vegetables were roasting on) to place the second pizza on, and bake both pizzas simultaneously, or you can bake them individually.

10. Pop the pizzas in the oven for about 12 minutes, until the cheese has melted and the crust is golden.

ANTIPASTO SALAD

After all of the amazing pasta and pizza options, it's definitely time to add in a healthy, refreshing, and light salad option. This antipasto salad is an extremely versatile meal, as it can serve as a healthy lunch option or accompany another dish at the dinner table. It's also a perfect salad option for a summer's Saturday BBQ. The literal definition of "antipasto" refers to a dish that comes before the rest, so this salad option can take on many different roles. It's also a quick salad to whip up if you're short for time and is sufficiently filling.

Difficulty Level: 4
Preparation Time: 10 minutes
Cooking Time: 5 minutes
Total Time: 15 minutes

Nutritional Info Per Serving Servings: 6	
Calories	379
Carbohydrates	3.9g
Fat	34.6g
Protein	14.5g

Estimated Budget: $4.00

Ingredients:

For the salad:

- 2 large romaine hearts, chopped thinly
- ½ cup of sliced olives
- ½ lb salami, sliced thinly
- 8 oz of mozzarella balls, cut in halves
- 1 cup of quartered artichoke hearts
- ¼ cup of mint leaves
- 1 cup of cherry tomatoes, chopped in halves
- 1 cup of chopped pepperoncini (banana peppers are a good substitute)

For the homemade vinaigrette:

- ½ cup of olive oil
- 1 tsp mustard seeds
- ¼ cup of red wine vinegar
- 1 tsp of Dijon mustard
- ½ tsp of oregano
- ½ tsp of chili flakes
- Salt & pepper to taste

Instructions:

1. Mix the lettuce, salami, artichokes, mozzarella, tomatoes, pepperoncini, olives, mint, and artichoke in a large salad bowl. If you have salad spoons, use this to mix the contents together; if

not, toss the contents in the bowl to have them integrate with each other.

2. For the vinaigrette, take a jar or container (anything that has a lid) and combine all of the ingredients: olive oil, mustard seeds, red wine vinegar, Dijon mustard, oregano, and chili flakes, and season with salt and pepper to taste. Stir the contents gently with a spoon/stirrer and close the container.

3. When serving the salad, stir the vinaigrette prior to drizzling over the salad (as the contents may have separated).

Chapter Five

GREEK DISHES

Similar to the Italian dishes, we've curated our five most favorite and famous Greek-style dishes. Through this journey, you'll come to see and understand how the spices and flavors work their way into Greek cuisine and quickly learn the more prominent flavors and aromas of this cuisine.

In Greek cuisine, they're famous for homing in on the art of tenderizing their meat to perfection through their spice combinations. Greek cuisine uses a lot of olive oil, Greek yogurt, chickpeas, and tzatziki. Their marinades are a prominent factor in their dishes, which is what makes their dishes stand out among the rest! Their ability to create perfectly flavored and tender-to-perfection meat is what we aim to explore within this chapter.

We've put together a top five list of meals that explore all options: poultry, vegetarian, roasts, red meat, salad, and even soup, just to explore how the spices and marinades are used in the different meals, thus enhancing the flavor and more so, the texture.

This collection of recipes is also inclusive of all occasions, from summer salads, to family dinners, to wintery soups. So, there is something for everyone, for any time.

In this chapter, you'll find the following recipes: a Greek salad and pita wedges, avgolemono chicken soup, gemista stuffed tomatoes, chicken gyros with tzatziki, and lamb chops (marinated to perfection) with roasted paidakia (potatoes). To add a further level of interest, we've included the traditional names for the meals so that you can familiarize yourself with them, their specific methods, ingredients, and flavors!

Again, in understanding the backstory to meals, it will help you to gain a whole other level of appreciation and enjoyment from the experience. As you go into this next chapter, keep an eye out for any dishes, ingredients, or methods that you really like, and try incorporating those methods or ingredients into other dishes that you make (this is when the cooking becomes fun and creative).

With the Greek cuisine, you'll be sure to find a lot of key ingredients such as olive oil. If you have the chance to swap your oil for olive oil, make this change, as it will enhance the taste in the meal so much more as well as provide a more Mediterranean feel to the dishes you make. Olive oil also comes with more health benefits than cooking with regular vegetable oil. Other key ingredients that you'll find in Greek dishes are herbs to spice the dishes. This includes herb mixes such as oregano, thyme, and rosemary (which are most common). You'll be sure to make use of a lot of tomatoes, cheeses, honey, olives, and Greek yogurt.

Try and look out for these ingredients within the recipes listed below and take note of how they work into the other ingredients to enhance the flavors and aromas. As mentioned above, Greek yogurt and marinade are great as they are able to beautifully tenderize the meat so that you enjoy a soft, succulent, and juicy dish!

If you come across any flavors or spices that you might take a liking to, make a note of them and incorporate them into your other meals. Experiment with them and see how these spices work with different foods.

In saying this, let's take a look at the recipes we've put together and try to pinpoint which ones you might like to tackle.

GRILLED PITA & GREEK SALAD

In keeping with the salad theme, one of the most common types there is, is the Greek salad. Famously known as a filling, yet still light meal, the Greek salad is brought to life through the zesty dressing and spices and is paired with grilled pita to bring a little carbohydrate into the meal. From the Dijon mustard, to the olives, to the fresh lemon juice, this recipe will make you feel as though you're on a Mediterranean island.

Difficulty Level: 2
Preparation Time: 15 minutes
Cooking Time: 10 minutes
Total Time: 25 minutes

Nutritional Info Per Serving Servings: 4	
Calories	396
Carbohydrates	48g
Fat	19g
Protein	12g

Estimated Budget: $6.00

Ingredients:

- 1 red bell pepper, sliced thinly, lengthwise
- ¼ cup of olive oil, divided
- 2 tsps of oregano
- ½ tsp of garlic powder
- ⅜ tsp of salt, divided
- 3 whole wheat pitas (about 6" each)
- 1 tbsp lemon juice
- 1 tbsp white wine vinegar
- 2 tsps of Dijon mustard
- ¼ tsp black pepper
- ¼ tsp chili flakes
- 4 cups of romaine lettuce, chopped
- 2 cups of English cucumber, chopped
- 1 cup of cherry tomatoes, halved
- 2 tbsps of pitted olives, chopped
- 1 can of cannellini beans, rinsed and drained
- ¼ cup of crumbled feta cheese

Instructions:

1. In a medium pan, heat a bit of oil over medium heat and add the peppers into the pan. Stir the slices around to coat them in oil and fry for about 2 minutes until soft. Remove from the pan and set aside. Keep the heat on the stove, as you're going to need it again in the next step.

2. Next, mix 1 tbsp of olive oil, 1 tsp of oregano, garlic powder, and a pinch of salt in a small bowl.

Brush the oil mixture over the pitas and place them onto the pan, cooking for 2 minutes on either side. Once the pitas are lightly toasted, set them aside and cut each pita into 6 equal wedges.

3. Lastly, get a large salad bowl out and add your salad ingredients: your pepper, lettuce, cucumber, olives, and tomatoes. Then drizzle 3 tbsps of olive oil into the bowl, along with the vinegar, lemon juice, and mustard. Season the salad with the remaining salt, pepper, and chili flakes. Use salad tongs or spoons, or simply toss the bowl's contents to mix all of the ingredients and flavors together.

4. Crumble Feta on top of the salad and serve with grilled pita wedges.

AVGOLEMONO CHICKEN SOUP

For a more hearty, warm, and homely meal, soup is always a good call. Avgolemono is a traditional soup that stems from the Greek cuisine. It's a combination of chicken broth and lemon juice–giving you a great protein boost with a zesty, lemony kick. This soup is a fantastic option for a cold, winter's day, or if you're feeling a little under the weather and need a good energy boosting meal. It's also an easy and quick dish to whip up, so it's perfect for if you don't have too much energy to cook.

Difficulty Level: 4
Preparation Time: 5 minutes
Cooking Time: 25 minutes
Total Time: 30 minutes

Nutritional Info Per Serving	
Calories	427
Carbohydrates	77.6g
Fat	2.5g
Protein	20.9

Estimated Budget: $5.00

Ingredients:

- 4 cups of chicken broth/stock
- 2 cups of white rice
- 2 egg yolks
- ⅓ cup of lemon juice
- 1 pound of boneless chicken, preferably breast pieces
- 1 tbsp of garlic & ginger paste
- ¼ cup of dill
- ¼ cup of cream (optional for drizzling)
- ¼ cup of melted butter

Instructions:

1. Start by cooking the rice. Pour the rice into a medium pot and fill with just enough water that it covers the rice. Set the rice to boil on medium-high heat for about 10 minutes (check the rice to see if it has softened).

2. While the rice cooks, prepare the chicken. Place a medium skillet on medium-high heat and drizzle a little bit of oil in the pan. Place the chicken breasts on a chopping board and cut them into thin slices, then add into the pan with the ginger and garlic paste. Stir the pieces around so that they are coated in the paste. As the chicken starts to cook, use two forks to pull the meat apart and shred the chicken. Let the meat cook for about 5

minutes until it's fully white and there's no more pink bits, then set aside.

3. Once the rice has cooked, drain it and set it aside.

4. In another pan over medium heat, add the stock/broth into the pan with salt and pepper. Bring the contents to a simmer and then take 1 cup of the hot stock and pour it into a blender. Add ½ a cup of rice, the 2 egg yolks, and lemon juice. Blend the contents until it turns into a smooth purée. Pour the purée back into the stock that's on the stove and add the shredded chicken in. Then, add the remaining 1 ½ cups of rice and dill into the pan and stir. Leave the contents to simmer for about 10 minutes, until thickened.

5. Serve in bowls and drizzle a little cream and melted butter on the soup for extra creaminess (optional).

GEMISTA – STUFFED TOMATOES

This traditional Greek recipe, gemista, is filled with fun and flavor! It's the perfect addition to a dinner get-together or, alternatively, you can enjoy this as a meal on its own. Gemista is another recipe that you can fine tune to your liking. Stuffed tomatoes are usually filled with rice and vegetables, but you can also add ground meat into them, if you'd like. You can serve them on their own (as a side dish), or add them to a pasta, a bed of rice, or even a salad. The possibilities are endless and the flavors are glorious. The most exciting trait that comes with gemistas is that the contents within the tomatoes are baked inside the tomato, so when you cut into them, you're welcomed with tangy aromas of the cooking vessel. The juice of the tomato also gloriously soaks into the rest of the contents that are stuffed within it, providing a seamless relationship between all of the ingredients.

Difficulty Level: 9
Preparation Time: 45 minutes
Cooking Time: 1 hour 15 minutes
Total Time: 2 hours

Nutritional Info Per Serving Servings: 14	
Calories	493

Carbohydrates	73.8g
Fat	20.6g
Protein	9.7g

Estimated Budget: $6.00

Ingredients:

- 8 tomatoes
- 1 eggplant
- 6 potatoes, chopped into wedges
- 4 green bell peppers
- 2 red onions, diced
- 1 tbsp of garlic paste
- 1 zucchini, chopped into cubes
- 2 cups of rice
- 1 can of chopped tomatoes
- 2 tbsps of tomato purée
- 2 tsps of sugar
- 2 tbsps of butter
- Salt & pepper to taste
- A pinch of parsley, chopped
- A pinch of mint, chopped
- Olive oil
- Feta cheese for sprinkling on top

Instructions:

Note: when cutting the tops off of the vegetables, do not discard them as you'll be using them in the recipe.

1. Chop the tops off of all of the tomatoes and spoon out the flesh inside of them–keep the flesh in a separate bowl, as you'll be making use of this soon.
2. Chop off the tops of the eggplants and spoon out their flesh too. Chop the flesh into small cubes and set aside for later.
3. Cut the top of the bell peppers off and remove the flesh and seeds from the inside (you can discard these).
4. Place the vegetable shells on a baking tray and season them with salt and sugar and place a little pinch of butter in the bottom of each of the vegetable shells. Set aside.
5. Now to prepare the gemista sauce: pour the flesh of the tomatoes into a blender with 5 tbsps of olive oil, tomato purée, the remaining sugar, salt, and pepper. Blend until well combined, then set aside.
6. Preheat the oven to 400°F.
7. For the gemista filling, place a medium saucepan over medium-high heat and drizzle in some olive oil. Add the onions and fry for about 5 minutes, stirring regularly, until the onions have browned. Then, add in the cubes of zucchini and sauté for

another minute. Pour in the cubes of eggplant flesh and garlic paste. Stir for another minute, then add in the rice and continue to sauté. Pour in the can of chopped tomatoes and add a pinch of salt and pepper. Stir well, for about 5 minutes. Once the liquid has evaporated, remove the pan from the heat and add in the parsley and mint.

8. In an ovenproof dish, place the vegetable shells, hollow side facing up, and spoon the tomato and rice mixture into each vegetable. Place the potato wedges in between the vegetable shells. Sprinkle salt and pepper once more over the vegetables, then pour the tomato sauce (from the blender) over the vegetables. Finally, cover the vegetable shells with their significant top pieces and then pour 2-3 glasses of water into the dish.

9. Cover the dish with foil and place in the oven for 1 hour. Remove the foil and leave the dish to bake for another 15 minutes.

10. Sprinkle feta cheese over the dish and serve! Gemistas can be enjoyed warm or cold (perfect for any weather).

CHICKEN GYROS & TZATZIKI

Traditional gyros' marinade offers a creamy, zesty, and herb flavor, stemming from the mix of Greek yogurt, garlic, and lemon. It's a perfect balance between a healthy intake of protein while still leaving you feeling filled and light. It's perfect as a summer's day lunch option and also a great option for meal prepping lunches for work. The most exciting factor that is attached to Greek cuisine (especially this recipe) is that the ingredients that are typically found in their dishes tenderize the meat while still offering a flavorsome experience. You'll often find that the meat in Greek cuisine is so tender and juicy–the ingredients play a key role in this aspect.

Note: the marinade for this recipe should be made in advance, to have the best taste and results. Try to prepare and marinate your meat the night before/the morning of, as it should take about 3 hours minimum to marinate. Also, note that you should not marinate for more than 24 hours.

Difficulty Level: 7
Preparation Time: 20 minutes (excluding marinade: 3 hours)
Cooking Time: 6 minutes
Total Time: 26 minutes

Nutritional Info Per Serving Servings: 4-6	
Calories	641.78
Carbohydrates	47.64g
Fat	20.26g
Protein	64.69g

Estimated Budget: $8.00

Ingredients:

- 2 lb of boneless chicken (preferably thigh/breast pieces)

Marinade ingredients:

- 2 tbsps of garlic paste
- 1 tbsp of white wine vinegar
- 3 tbsps of lemon juice
- 1 tbsp of olive oil
- 3 tbsps of Greek yogurt
- 1 ½ tbsps of dried oregano
- Salt and pepper to taste (about ½ tsp of each should be enough)

Tzatziki ingredients:

- 2 cucumbers
- 1 ¼ cups of Greek yogurt
- 1 tbsp of lemon juice
- 1 tbsp of olive oil
- ½ tbsp of garlic paste
- A pinch of mint
- Salt and pepper to taste (about ¼ tsp of each should be enough)

Greek salad ingredients:

- 3 cucumbers, diced
- 3 tomatoes, deseeded and diced
- ½ of a red onion, peeled and sliced thinly
- ¼ cup of parsley
- ⅕ cup of mint
- Pita bread for serving (optional)

Instructions:

1. Combine all of the marinade ingredients into a plastic bag: the garlic paste, white wine vinegar, lemon juice, olive oil, Greek yogurt, oregano, salt, and pepper. Place the chicken pieces into the bag and massage the meat so that the juices and spices work into the meat. Set the meat aside/in the refrigerator (if it's a hot day) and let it marinate

for at least 3-12 hours, however, not more than 24 hours.

2. When the meat is almost ready, prepare the tzatziki. Cut the cucumbers in half, lengthwise, and spoon out the watery, seeded center parts. Grate the cucumber and then wrap the grated cucumber in a paper towel to draw out all of the extra moisture.

3. In a small bowl, add the grated cucumber with the rest of the tzatziki ingredients: Greek yogurt, lemon juice, olive oil, garlic paste, mint, salt, and pepper. Mix the contents well and place in the refrigerator.

4. For the salad, wash all of the vegetables, dice them, and add them into a medium bowl. Use salad tongs or spoons to mix well.

5. Once your chicken has marinated, remove the meat from the bag (keep the marinade as you will use it again just now), and place the meat in a medium pan over medium-high heat and drizzle 1 tbsp of oil into the pan. Fry for about 2-3 minutes on each side until golden brown (if the chicken pieces are bigger, you may need to cook them for up to 5 minutes on either side). Set the chicken pieces aside to cool.

6. Cut your chicken pieces into strips. Lay the pita bread on foil (the piece of foil should be a little bigger than the pita bread). Spoon some salad down the middle of the pita, then add a few pieces of chicken and tzatziki.

7. Roll the pita up, with the help of the foil, and twist the bottom end of the foil.

LAMB CHOPS & POTATO PAIDAKIA

Paidakia originated in Greece and is still considered a staple dish in their cuisine. Similar to the chicken gyros, this delectable dish of lamb chops will also require an extra bit of time to allow the chops to properly marinate—but, as usual, it is worth it! Allowing the meat to properly tenderize in the marinade will create a succulent dish full of savory, spicy flavors and aromas Perfect for a family dinner or get-together, this meal is a more filling, homely meal, fit for the special occasions.

Note: this recipe needs at least 3 hours' worth of marinating time. Preferably, you should try to marinate it earlier in the morning or the night before, but aim to at least have 3 hours' worth of marinating time.

Difficulty Level: 5
Preparation Time: 3 hours (incl. marinating time)
Cooking Time: 1 hours 30 minutes
Total Time: 4 hours 30 minutes

Nutritional Info Per Serving Servings: 4	
Calories	708
Carbohydrates	37.3g

Fat	46.3g
Protein	40.4g

Estimated Budget: $15.00

Ingredients:

To prepare the marinade:

- 8 lamb ribs (about 1 ½ lbs)
- ⅓ cup of olive oil
- 1 tbsp of garlic paste
- 1 ½ tbsps of mustard
- 1 tbsp of thyme, chopped finely
- 1 tbsp of rosemary, chopped
- ½ tsp of oregano
- 3 peppercorns
- ½ lemon's zest
- ½ tsp of salt

To prepare the potatoes:

- 4 medium-sized potatoes, cut into wedges
- 1 tbsp of garlic paste
- ¼ cup of olive oil
- Juice of 1 whole lemon
- ½ tsp of semolina
- 1 tsp of oregano
- ½ tsp of rosemary

- ⅓ cup of water
- Salt & pepper to taste

Instructions:

1. For the marinade, grab a large bowl and pour all of the marinade ingredients into it: olive oil, garlic paste, mustard, thyme, rosemary, oregano, peppercorns, lemon zest, and salt. Mix well to combine all of the ingredients. Place the lamb chops into the marinade and, using your hands, massage the marinade into the meat. Make sure to massage the spices into the meat well, to get the flavors to work their way deep into the meat. Cover the bowl with plastic wrap or a lid, and place it in the refrigerator to marinate for at least 3 hours (if you can leave it longer or prepare it the night before, this is preferable).

2. Once the chops have marinated, remove them from the refrigerator and allow them to level to room temperature (about 20 minutes at least).

3. Preheat the oven to 200°F.

4. While the chops are reaching room temperature, prepare the potatoes. In a small bowl, combine the ingredients for the potatoes: the garlic paste, olive oil, lemon juice, semolina, oregano, rosemary, water, salt, and pepper. Stir well to combine, then set aside.

5. Prepare a baking tray and lay the potato wedges out on the tray. Evenly pour the mixture in the

small bowl onto the wedges. Use a spoon/fork to shuffle the wedges around the mixture so as to evenly coat them. Sprinkle a little more salt and pepper onto the wedges and then pop the tray into the oven for 40 minutes.

6. Once the wedges are a nice golden brown in color and crusted around the edges, remove them from the oven and sprinkle them with a little more salt and oregano. Give the tray a little toss and shake, to mix the seasoning with the wedges. Check if the liquid in the tray has dried out, add another ¼ cup of warm water into the pan, then pop the tray back into the oven for another 30 minutes.

7. While the potatoes are roasting, prepare the paidakia (lamb chops): remove the chops from the marinade and place them on a baking tray. Sprinkle the chops with a pinch of salt and pepper and place in the oven for 20-25 minutes. Check on the chops halfway through, turning them over and pour a little of the marinade over them to tenderize them more.

8. Once the wedges and paidakia are ready, allow them to cool for about 5 minutes, then squeeze a few drops of lemon juice over the paidakia, and season with more oregano. Serve warm.

Chapter Six

PORTUGUESE DISHES

Working with Portuguese cuisine is both tricky and exciting on another level. It's tricky because Portuguese dishes work with a lot of seafood, so if you're not experienced with cooking seafood, it might seem a little scary or confusing at first. However, once you dive right into the dishes, you'll soon realize how truly exciting and invigorating the experience is. By throwing yourself in the deep end (or unfamiliar territory), you'll soon notice how easy the methods really are and how efficient the dishes are in regard to how the seafood is spiced and cooked, through the process of preparing the actual dish. Once you get the hang of how to properly work with the seafood, you'll start to see how easy the whole process is.

The majority of the work when handling the seafood is actually the cleaning process. You need to make sure that you've taken enough time out beforehand to properly clean, descale, devein, etc., the fish and shellfish. Thereafter, the cooking process is easy as pie! And in following the methods of these dishes, you'll notice that the steps are specifically placed to help you cook the fish in the most efficient manner, while preparing the rest of the meal (and we love efficiency).

The recipes that are included in this chapter, which are once again curated and narrowed down to five main dishes, are the following: Portuguese fish stew (caldeirada de peixe), prego piri piri, paella (which is a mix of seafood in rice), shrimp and chorizo (a divine, rich, and flavorful dish), and lastly, prawn cakes.

As you've noticed, we have once again made use of some of the traditional names of the meals, which you can familiarize yourself with. We hope that you explore this more challenging chapter with a curious mind, as the rich, flavorful Portuguese cuisine and its dishes are so very worth the challenge!

If you're able to master a few of these recipes at home, you've mastered one of the more challenging chapters in this copycat recipe book. Here's wishing you all the luck, and happy cooking!

Similar to the above-mentioned cuisines, Italian and Greek, Portuguese cuisine also has a few key ingredients and spices that you should keep an eye out for.

Portuguese dishes love to usually start off with a bay leaf in the mix, as it brings out an herb flavor and aroma prior to preparing the dish. Bay leaves are also high in Vitamin A and iron, so by starting off the dish by frying a bay leaf into the spice mix, it will not only add aromas and fragrance to the dish, but it will also incorporate a few vitamin boosts into the base mix.

Portuguese cuisine also tends to incorporate chili flakes or piri piri sauce into its dishes to add an extra level of zest and a spicy kick to the meal. Some dishes are quite spicy (therefore the Portuguese rolls help to curb the spiciness). We have included a recipe for a homemade piri piri sauce into the Prego Roll recipe, although there are various variations of piri piri sauces. Piri piri sauce was first created by the African Portuguese culture, and it was then later adopted by Australians who found out that the sauce worked well with flame grilled meat (on the BBQ).

Lastly, make sure to keep an eye out for paprika spice; this spice gives off a lovely smoked, sweet aroma and taste. You do get a spicier paprika that is also commonly used, but the sweeter paprika is widely used in many Portuguese dishes. Keep an eye out for which dishes make use of this spice and what it does to enhance the flavors and ingredients.

Now that you've got a good understanding of the key Portuguese ingredients and spices, let's get into the recipes!

CALDEIRA DE PEIXI (FISH STEW)

Portuguese cuisine is most famous for its zesty, tangy and spicy flavors, which go especially well with white meat–chicken and fish. This Portuguese fish stew is a glorious mix of seafood and spice. If you're in the mood for some seafood, this will definitely comfort those cravings. This recipe yields 6-8 servings, so it's perfect for a family dinner or entertaining a few friends.

Difficulty Level: 6
Preparation Time: 30 minutes (for cleaning the fish & vegetables)
Cooking Time: 30 minutes
Total Time: 1 hour

Nutritional Info Per Serving Servings: 6-8	
Calories	389
Carbohydrates	38.2g
Fat	4.4g
Protein	38.2g

Estimated Budget: $15.00-$17.00

Ingredients:

- 2 onions, chopped thinly
- 1 red bell pepper, deseeded and diced
- 1 red chili, chopped thinly
- 2 whole cloves of garlic
- 1 tbsp of chopped coriander
- 14 oz. of dry white wine
- 1 bay leaf
- 10 oz of potatoes, peeled and cubed
- 1 can of whole tomatoes
- A pinch of saffron
- 21 oz of skinless white fish, cut into chunks
- 10 oz of squid, cleaned and sliced
- 6-8 tiger prawns, cleaned, deveined, and sliced
- 1 lb of clams, cleaned
- 1 lb of mussels, cleaned
- 1 baguette, cut into slices
- 1 tbsp of garlic paste
- A pinch of mixed herbs spice
- ½ tbsp of butter
- Parmesan for sprinkling (optional)
- Olive oil for drizzling

Instructions:

1. In a large frying pan (with a lid/cover), drizzle a little olive oil and bring to a medium heat. Add the onion in and fry until softened, about 2 minutes. Finely chop 2 garlic cloves into the pan

and add the coriander and chili. Stir well and fry for another 3 minutes, until fragrant.

2. Pour the wine, bay leaf, and saffron into the pan and reduce the heat to medium low. Allow to simmer until the liquid is reduced to half the amount.

3. Once the liquid has reduced, add the cubes of potato, tomatoes, and ½ a cup of water. Bring the contents to a boil, stirring regularly to break up the tomatoes and mix the contents. Leave the contents to simmer for another 20-25 minutes, until the potatoes are just tender (you can pierce them with a fork to check if they've softened).

4. Taste the sauce to check for seasoning, adding more salt to your taste. Add in the fish and then layer the squid, prawns, clams, and mussels on the top layer (try not to soak them too much in the sauce, aim to have the fish chunks at the base). Cover the pan and cook for 6-8 minutes until the shells of the clams and mussels have opened, the prawns have reddened in color, and the fish is flaky–these are all signs that the dish is fully cooked and ready.

5. While the fish stew is cooking, prepare the baguette. On each slice of the baguette, add a bit of butter and garlic paste, and season with mixed herbs seasoning. Toast the slices, either in a toaster, in the oven or on a stove top. Lightly drizzle olive oil over the top of the slices.

6. Serve the stew with baguette toasted slices. Garnish the stew with coriander and sprinkle with parmesan.

PIRI PIRI PREGO

Prego rolls are another favorite meal that roots itself in Portugal; they're simply a level up from your normal, everyday sandwich. It's bursting with flavors and nutrition. This recipe combines spicy piri piri sauce with a hearty meat option. You can always substitute the meat with something else to your preferred diet/taste. This is the perfect lunch option as it's wholesome, filling, and absolutely delicious–it's definitely a meal that will get you through any day.

Note: this recipe also requires some time for the meat to marinate (if you're using); consider marinating the meat the morning of/the night before. The minimum time that you should aim to marinate the meat for is 1 hour at *least*.

Difficulty Level: 3
Preparation Time: 2 hours 20 minutes (for marinating)
Cooking Time: 10 minutes
Total Time: 2 hours 30 minutes

Nutritional Info Per Serving Servings: 2	
Calories	636
Carbohydrates	46.7g
Fat	29.9g

Protein	42.8g

Estimated Budget: $12.00

Ingredients:

- 1 tbsp of garlic paste
- 2 small rump steaks (about ⅓ lb each)
- 2 tbsp of olive oil
- 1 tbsp of sherry vinegar
- ¼ cup of parsley
- ¼ cup of rocket
- 2 ciabatta rolls, toasted
- ¼ cup of crumbled Feta cheese

For the piri piri sauce:

- 1 jalapeño, chopped
- 1 tsp of chopped mint
- 1 tbsp of sherry vinegar
- 2 spring onions, chopped finely
- ½ a garlic clove, chopped finely
- 1 tsp of sugar
- ⅕ cup of basil
- ⅕ cup of parsley

Instructions:

1. Massage the steaks well with the garlic paste; try to coat the steaks well so that the garlic works its

way into the meat. Place the steaks into a plastic bag along with the olive oil, sherry vinegar, and parsley. Once more, massage everything together, through the plastic bag, then close the bag tightly and roll over the steaks with a rolling pin. Leave the meat to marinate for 1-2 hours at least (if it's a hot day, place the meat in the refrigerator).

2. Using a blender, combine all of the sauce ingredients: the chopped jalapeño, mint, sherry vinegar, spring onions, garlic clove, sugar, basil, and parsley. Pour in 1 tbsp of water and blend until smooth. Pour the sauce into a container or jar and store in the refrigerator to cool down.

3. Once the meat is nicely marinated, heat up a pan over medium-high heat. Place the steaks individually onto the pan and season once more with a pinch of salt. Sear the steaks for about 2 minutes on either side and then set aside.

4. Slice the steaks into strips and place them into your toasted ciabatta buns. Add the sauce and more rocket. Crumble Feta cheese into each roll, and enjoy!

PAELLA

Although paella originated in Spain, Spain does share some similar cultural traits with Portuguese culture and tradition. This traditional dish has been a massive attraction for tourists. Paella is a quick, flavorful dish to make that's filling and wholesome. It serves 6 and can be made in under an hour. It's perfect for a family dinner or to incorporate into your meal prepping for the week. Not only is it a delicious combination of protein, vegetables and carbs, it also yields quite a good amount of servings for the time put into making it—so make sure when you prepare this dish, you can put it to good use!

Difficulty Level: 7
Preparation Time: 20 minutes
Cooking Time: 25 minutes
Total Time: 45 minutes

Nutritional Info Per Serving Servings: 6	
Calories	335.6
Carbohydrates	47.6g
Fat	4.9g
Protein	23.5g

Estimated Budget: $7.00

Ingredients:

- 6 boneless chicken thighs/breast pieces
- 1 link of Portuguese chourico, sliced
- ¼ tsp of rosemary spice
- 1 cup of onions, diced
- ½ cup of bell pepper, diced
- 1 ½ cups of uncooked rice
- ½ cup of diced tomato
- 1 tsp of paprika
- ¼ tsp of saffron
- 1 tbsp of garlic paste, divided
- 3 cups of chicken broth
- ¾ lb of shrimp, peeled, deveined, and cleaned
- 1 cup of asparagus, cut diagonally
- ½ cup of peas
- Salt & pepper to taste
- Oil for coating the surface of the pan
- ½ cup of cream
- 1 tbsp of melted butter

Instructions:

1. Preheat your oven to 400°F and heat about 2 tbsps of oil in a medium-large skillet/oven proof pan over medium-high heat.
2. Season the chicken pieces with rosemary, ½ tbsp of garlic paste, salt, and pepper to taste. Mix the

seasoning with the chicken, making sure that it's nicely coated. Place the chicken into the pot and cook for about 5 minutes on either side, until it's light brown on the surface.

3. Remove the chicken from the pan and set aside. Place the chourico into the pan and cook for about 5-8 minutes until lightly brown, stirring regularly so that it doesn't stick to the pan.

4. Add the bell pepper and onion and cook for another 5 minutes, stirring regularly until the onions have softened.

5. Pour the rice, tomato, paprika, saffron, and remaining garlic into the pan and cook for another 1 minute, still stirring.

6. Add the chicken back into the pan, along with the broth and a pinch of salt. Bring the contents to a boil.

7. Cover the pan with foil and pop into the oven to bake for 10 minutes.

8. Add the shrimp, asparagus, and peas into the pan and shake the pan. Cover the pan once more and place into the oven to bake for another 5-8 minutes (until the shrimp are no longer transparent).

9. While the contents are baking, mix together the cream and melted butter in a small bowl.

10. Pour the cream mixture over the dish, once it's done baking. Serve warm.

QUICK QUESTION:

Are you enjoying the recipes so far? Have they interested you and provided some insight on understanding the relationship between spices, flavors, aromas, and the meal itself?

If you have been enjoying this cookbook so far, please do consider leaving us a review when you're done, as we'd love to hear from you!

Let us know what recipes you've tried and which recipes you want to try! Tell us how they turned out and if you've done anything differently or even adopted a new staple ingredient into your grocery pantry! The options are endless.

Our goal with *Copycat Recipes* is to help inspire you to get cooking and make the foods that you love, unique to *you*! Let us know how your journey has been going thus far, and if you'd like to see more of these recipes, or any others.

Thank you again, so much, for choosing *Copycat Recipes* to assist you along your cooking journey!

Happy cooking, and more importantly, happy eating!

SHRIMP & CHORIZO

This Portuguese-inspired dish is a rich combination of shrimp and chorizo. It's perfect for a fancier night or if you'd like to impress your friends (or someone you fancy!). It's a quick and easy recipe but oozes with juicy flavor from the chorizo. Combined with the richness of the shrimp and tangy flavors of the tomatoes, it's definitely an impressive dish to treat yourself/your guests with.

Difficulty Level: 5
Preparation Time: 20 minutes
Cooking Time: 20 minutes
Total Time: 40 minutes

Nutritional Info Per Serving Servings: 4	
Calories	574
Carbohydrates	24.5g
Fat	28.9g
Protein	54.6g

Estimated Budget: $10.00

Ingredients:

- 1 tbsp of olive oil
- 8 ounces of chorizo (remove the casing and slice)
- 1 potato, peeled and chopped
- 1 carrot, peeled and chopped
- 2 tbsps of garlic paste
- 1 Fresno pepper
- 1 bay leaf
- 1 cup of kale, chopped
- 2 tbsps of thyme
- 1 tsp of ground nutmeg
- 1 can of chickpeas, drained
- 1 can of tomatoes, diced
- 3 cups of chicken stock
- 1 ½ pounds of shrimp, deveined, and cleaned
- Juice of 1 lemon
- Portuguese rolls to serve with

Instructions:

1. In a medium pot, heat up 1 tbsp of olive oil over medium heat. Place the chorizo into the pot and cook for 2 minutes, stirring regularly so that the chorizo doesn't stick to the bottom.
2. Pour the potatoes, onion, carrot, garlic paste, Fresno pepper, thyme, and bay leaf into the pot and cook for about 6 minutes, stirring regularly.

3. Check for the tenderness of the onions and potatoes, then add in the kale and nutmeg. Stir for another minute until the kale has wilted.

4. Pour the chickpeas, tomatoes, and stock into the pot and bring to a boil over medium-high heat. Then reduce the heat to a simmer.

5. Season with salt and pepper to taste and allow to simmer for 2 minutes.

6. Add in the shrimp and stir for about 5 minutes until the shrimp is pink in color. Stir in the lemon juice then remove from heat.

7. Serve the meal in shallow bowls and drizzle a little olive oil over each serving. Add in a Portuguese roll and serve hot.

PRAWN CAKES

Serve as an appetizer or along with other dishes as an accompaniment. Whatever the occasion is, prawn cakes are always a successful hit. Crunchy, rich, and seasoned to perfection, these Portuguese-inspired prawn deep-fried pastries are an entire experience on its own! Though it is a bit time consuming to prepare (about 2 hours), this recipe also yields quite a good number of servings: 12, to be precise. This recipe is perfect for special occasions, festive seasons, or social gatherings. Or if you simply want to spoil yourself, you can prepare this as a treat to last you a few days.

Difficulty Level: 9-10
Preparation Time: 30 minutes
Cooking Time: 40 minutes
Total Time: 1 hour 10 minutes

Nutritional Info Per Serving Servings: 6	
Calories	323
Carbohydrates	19.8g
Fat	15.2g
Protein	16.1g

Estimated Budget: $10.00

Ingredients:

- 1 ⅓ lbs of whole prawns, deveined and cleaned
- 1 ½ cups of milk
- 2 bay leaves
- 3-4 tbsps of butter
- ½ small onion, cut into thin slices
- ½ tbsp of garlic paste
- 1 tomato, peeled, deseeded, and diced
- ½ tbsp of coriander
- ½ tbsp of parsley
- 1 tsp of cayenne pepper
- ½ tsp of paprika
- ¼ tsp of nutmeg
- ½ tsp of mixed herbs spice
- 2 tbsps of cornstarch
- 1 lemon (for its juice and wedges for serving)
- 3 eggs
- ¼ cup of breadcrumbs
- Oil for frying
- Salt and pepper to taste (about ½ tsp of each)

To prepare the pastry:

- 2 tbsps of butter (unsalted preferably; if salted, remove salt from this ingredient list)
- 1 tsp salt
- 1 tsp of white pepper

- ½ tsp of paprika
- ¼ tsp of cayenne pepper
- ⅓ cup of all-purpose flour

Instructions:

1. Preheat the oven to 350°F and heat up a large pan (with a lid) on the stove.
2. Add the prawns, milk, and bay leaves into the pan and stir slowly. Once the milk is somewhat steaming, leave the prawns to cook in it for about 4-5 minutes.
3. Remove the pan from the heat and remove the prawns from the pan and place on a separate plate. Deshell and remove the heads from the prawns once they've cooled down (place the shells and heads in a roasting tin/oven dish), then chop the prawns up into small chunks.
4. Drizzle oil over the shells and heads then roast for 10-15 minutes in the oven. Once the shells and heads have pinkened in color and are fragrant, add them back into the pan with the milk and heat the pan again, until the milk is steaming once again. Then remove from heat and cover the pan, leaving the pan's contents to infuse with each other, for about 30 minutes.
5. After 30 minutes, strain the milk through a sieve and into a cup. Press the shells and heads against the sieve to squeeze out the remaining flavor then discard all of them.

6. You should have about 25 oz of liquid; you can add more milk into the cup if it's under this amount. Reserve about ⅓ of the milk, and pour the rest back into the pan.

7. Add 2 tbsps of butter, salt, pepper, and paprika to the pan with the milk, bringing the contents to a low-medium heat.

8. While the contents are heating, sift the flour into the pan and then whisk the contents, using a whisk. Keep whisking until a dough is formed.

9. Transfer the dough onto a lightly floured working surface.

10. Give the dough about a minute to cool down and then knead into it. Halve the dough and place each half in a bowl, cover it, and leave to cool to room temperature.

11. In the interim, make the filling. In another pan, melt the butter and fry the onion until browned and soft. Then add in the garlic and cook for another minute. Pour the tomatoes into the pan and stir for 2-3 minutes. Now, add in the remaining infused milk that you reserved, along with coriander, parsley, cayenne, salt, paprika, nutmeg, and mixed herb spice.

12. In another small bowl, mix your cornstarch with 2 tbsps of water and create a smooth paste. Pour the paste into the milk and stir until the mixture is thick.

13. Add in the chopped prawn meat and a squeeze of lemon juice, then remove from heat.

14. On a lightly floured surface, roll out the dough. Using a round pastry cutter (or an upside-down mug), cut circles into the dough; you should end up with about 36 circles altogether.

15. In a separate, small bowl, beat 1 egg yolk.

16. Dollop 1 tsp of prawn filling in the center of each circle and then coat the circumference of the circles with the yolk. Fold the circle pastries over to create semi-circles and then press the edges down with your fingers, so that the filling is secure.

17. Place the pastries on a baking tray lined with parchment paper/cooking spray.

18. Then crack the last 2 eggs into a bowl and whisk. In another bowl, pour the breadcrumbs. Dip each pastry into the egg and then into the breadcrumbs, then place it back onto the tray.

19. Drizzle oil into another large saucepan and bring it to a medium-high temperature. Place each pastry in and fry for 6-8 minutes, flipping them over once, halfway.

20. Once they are golden brown, place on a paper towel to drain the extra oil and then sprinkle with salt. Garnish with parsley and serve with lemon wedges.

Chapter Seven

VEGAN

This chapter aims to make the vegan diet even more exciting; not only is this chapter for strict vegans, it aims to also entice others who aren't, to try vegan dishes. This chapter aims to simply promote healthier meal options that are flavorful but won't leave you feeling tired, lethargic, and heavy.

In this chapter, we're going international!

Expect to pay a visit to the streets of Bombay, then hop on a plane to China, and then circle back around to Italy. All of this traveling in one chapter has already got us starving for some good food! The best part about all of this traveling and vast, diverse options is that you'll also gain an understanding of how places around the world spice and prepare their food, so that you're not merely getting healthy vegan options, you're also getting the experience, history, and flavors from around the world.

Similarly, to the idea that was emphasized in the Italian, Portuguese, and Greek cuisine chapters, understanding food's history, the key spices, the stories, and how the meals came about adds so much character to the meal and enhances the experience that much more. Subsequently, the same should also be applied to vegan dishes from around the world.

As mentioned in the vegetarian chapter, there's so many vast options and varieties of meals that vegetables can offer. If they're spiced and cooked properly, then there's so much potential with the dishes. The only downside is that franchises hardly offer much variety when it comes to vegetarian and vegan dishes, so it's often within our own hands to make our meals exciting. But this is a good thing, because that means that we can prepare the meals to our liking; for example, if you feel that you prefer oven-baked meals to frying vegetables, then you have control over this. You also have control over how you spice your own meals. It's essentially more cost-effective, healthier, tastier, and more unique to your liking. The only thing that you need to focus on with these diets is meal prepping in advance so that you don't end up eating boring/unhealthy substitutions.

In saying this, the list of five recipes that we have curated should add a little more spice (literally and metaphorically) to that diet. You'll notice that we've incorporated a dish from India, called the Bombay Burrito (also known as a roti roll). It originated as a dish on the streets of Bombay. It's a delicious, wholesome wrap that's filled with spices, chickpeas, a mint chutney, and yes, potato curry! This Bombay Burrito is the epitome of what an any-time meal is. You can enjoy it as a lunch at home, or on the go, or even have one for dinner. It can be enjoyed cold or warm… It's definitely a staple food to consider exploring. Next up, there is the Chinese eggplant. That's a crisp and salty dish that can be enjoyed on its own or be accompanied by a carb of your choice. Once you try this eggplant recipe, you'll definitely be craving it again soon. It's spiced to perfection and filling yet won't leave you feeling lethargic. It's also an incredibly quick and easy recipe to master.

Hopping back onto the Italian train, next up, we have a vegan Alfredo pasta. This delicious meal is definitely a foolproof dish for the more special occasions—it's creamy, filled with mushrooms and peas, and the epitome of a good, hearty meal. Not to mention, it's a quick recipe to whip up. The best part is that you won't even notice that it's a vegan dish—it's that delicious!

Last up, we have the quinoa cakes with relish. Referring back to the vegetarian chapter, we had also included a vegetarian patty recipe (because the lack of options for burgers at franchise fast-food outlets are quite limited). So, in light of this, we've added one more patty recipe, specified to the vegan diet. Not only does this recipe offer a route to making delicious patties, you've also got a saucy relish to go with it. This recipe is definitely the best of both worlds: it's healthy and it's delicious.

BOMBAY BURRITOS

Otherwise known as a roti roll/wrap, this Indian-inspired meal is perfect for any time of the day, whether you're on the go or relaxing at home. It can be enjoyed warm or cold—it's the perfect anytime meal. The best part is that it's bursting with flavor from the curried potatoes and mint chutney. You're getting a promising amount of healthy protein and iron intake, as there's a good amount of chickpeas and spinach too. You're bound to enjoy the flavorful experience in this recipe.

Difficulty Level: 5
Preparation Time: 30 minutes
Cooking Time: 30 minutes
Total Time: 1 hour

Nutritional Info Per Serving Servings: 4	
Calories	490
Carbohydrates	77.1g
Fat	15.6g
Protein	14.2g

Estimated Budget: $8.00

Ingredients:

For the curry potatoes:

- 16 ounces of baby potatoes, washed, peeled, & quartered
- 1 tbsp of olive oil
- 3 tbsps of curry powder
- 1 tbsp of turmeric
- ½ an onion, diced
- Salt to taste

For the filling:

- 1 head of cauliflower, separated into florets
- 1 can of chickpeas, drained
- 2 tbsps of olive oil
- 1 tbsp of coriander
- 1 tbsp of cumin
- 1 tsp of fennel seeds
- 1 tsp of coriander seeds
- Salt to taste
- ½ of a red onion, sliced thinly
- 2 cups of baby spinach
- 4 large tortillas/rotis (make sure that the wraps are vegan friendly, as some are made with ghee)

For the Cilantro Chutney:

- ½ cup of coconut/soy yogurt

- 3 tbsps of lemon juice
- ¼ cup of cilantro
- 1 cup of mint leaves
- 1 jalapeno, sliced
- 1 tsp of garlic paste
- ½ tsp of honey
- ½ tsp of salt

Instructions:

To prepare the Cilantro Chutney:

1. Blend all of the ingredients in a blender until smooth and store in a glass jar.

For the potatoes and filling:

1. Preheat the oven to 425°F and place a medium-large pot on the stove. Fill the pot halfway with water and add the potato chunks into the water. Bring the contents to a boil and cook for 15-20 minutes until the potatoes are tender.
2. While the potatoes boil, place the cauliflower florets and chickpeas onto a baking tray and lightly drizzle with olive oil. Season the cauliflower and chickpeas with salt, coriander, cumin, chili flakes (to taste), fennel seed, and coriander seeds. Toss the contents to mix them well and then pop in the oven for 20-25 minutes, turning them halfway through.

3. Once the potatoes are ready, drain about ¾ of the water out (save about 1 cups worth of water). Mash the potatoes with the water, salt, spices, and oil. Mash until you've formed a smooth paste.

4. Once the vegetables are almost done, warm up the tortillas in either the oven or over the stove.

5. Spread the potato spread down the center of the tortillas, then add in a spoonful of chickpeas, followed by some cauliflower florets. Cut up some baby spinach and layer it on top of the wraps, then add in a few slices of onion. Finally, dollop the Cilantro Chutney onto the burritos. Wrap it all together and enjoy!

CHINESE STYLE EGGPLANT AND SZECHUAN SAUCE

This spicy recipe is for both the lovers of spicy food and eggplant fans. The best part about this recipe is that the way that it is cooked will result in a lovely, crispy eggplant that's infused with tantalizingly spicy aromas and flavors. It's extremely easy to whip up, and it can work its way into so many different meals. You can enjoy it on its own or with a carb of your choice or add it into another meal! It's extremely versatile and delicious; it's safe to say this recipe should be a new staple in our diet.

Difficulty Level: 4

Preparation Time: 20 minutes

Cooking Time: 25 minutes

Total Time: 45 minutes

Nutritional Info Per Serving Servings: 4	
Calories	323
Carbohydrates	29.6g
Fat	21.8g

Protein	5.9g

Estimated Budget: $4.00

Ingredients:

- 1 ½ lbs of Japanese eggplant
- 2 tsps of salt
- 2 tbsps of cornstarch
- 3-4 tbsps of peanut oil
- 2 tbsps of garlic & ginger paste
- 5-10 dried, red chiles (depending on your preference)
- 2 scallions, chopped for garnish
- ½ cup of roasted peanuts/cashews for garnish

For the Szechuan sauce:

- 1 tsp of peppercorns (preferably Szechuan peppercorns)
- ¼ cup of soy sauce
- 1 tbsp of garlic paste
- 1 tbsp of chili flakes
- 1 tbsp of sesame oil
- 1 tbsp of rice vinegar
- 1 tbsp of mirin
- 3 tbsps of brown sugar or honey
- ½ tsp of five spice all spice

Instructions:

1. Chop the eggplant into chunks and place in a bowl filled with water. Add 2 tsps of salt and cover with a plate. Let it sit for about 30 minutes.

2. Make the Szechuan sauce in the meantime. Place a pan over medium heat and add in the peppercorns. Roast them on the dry pan for 1-2 minutes. Crush the peppercorns up and place into a bowl, along with the other ingredients: soy sauce, garlic paste, chili flakes, sesame oil, rice vinegar, mirin, brown sugar, and allspice. Whisk the ingredients together and set aside.

3. Once the eggplant is ready, drain the water and pat the eggplant dry with a paper towel. Add in the cornstarch and mix.

4. Heat a tbsp of oil in a wok/pan over medium heat and add half of the eggplant into the pan. Stir the eggplant so that it fries evenly. Fry the first batch for about 10 minutes, then repeat with the second batch. Make sure that the cooked eggplant is nice and brown. Set aside once cooked.

5. Add 1 more tbsp oil into the pan and add in the ginger and garlic paste and stir for about 2 minutes until the aromas awaken. Add the chiles into the pan (be sure to turn the fan of the stove on). Stir the chiles for about 1 minute and then pour in the Szechuan sauce. Stir for another 20-30 seconds and then finally add the eggplant back into the pan, mixing for another minute. If the

contents start to dry out, add in another tbsp of
water.

6. Garnish with chopped scallions and peanuts.

VEGAN ALFREDO

If you're looking for a more Italian-inspired dish or craving a little comfort food, this vegan Alfredo pasta will win your heart. Its creamy, zesty mixture that incorporates well into the mushrooms is what makes this dish so unique and special. Not to mention, it only takes a mere half an hour to whip up. So, you don't need to spend too much energy or time, but the end result is still so delicious!

Difficulty Level: 3
Preparation Time: 10 minutes
Cooking Time: 20 minutes
Total Time: 30 minutes

Nutritional Info Per Serving Servings: 2	
Calories	564
Carbohydrates	75.1g
Fat	21.2g
Protein	23g

Estimated Budget: $4.00

Ingredients:

- 1 cup of pasta of your choice (long, flat pasta is best, such as tagliatelle pasta)
- 1 cup of peas
- 8 ounces of mushrooms
- 1 tsp of chili flakes
- A pinch of parsley for garnish
- ¼ lemon zest for garnish

For the sauce:

- 1 tbsp of olive oil
- ½ onion, thinly sliced
- 4 whole cloves of garlic
- ½ cup of cashews
- 1 cup of vegetable broth
- 2 tbsps of yeast
- ½ tsp of miso paste
- ⅛ tsp of nutmeg
- Salt and pepper to taste

Instructions:

1. Boil the pasta in a large pot filled with water and a pinch of salt. Boil for about 10 minutes until the pasta has softened.
2. For the Alfredo sauce, place a pan over medium-low heat and drizzle in a little bit of oil. Add in the onions and garlic, frying for about 3-5 minutes until the onions are tender and fragrant.

3. Pop the onions and garlic into a blender with the cashews, vegetable broth, yeast, miso, salt, and nutmeg and blend for about 30 seconds-1 minute until the mixture is smooth.
4. Pour a little more oil into the pan and add in the mushrooms. Raise the heat to medium and sauté for 6-7 minutes, until the mushrooms are tender. Season with salt and pepper to taste.
5. Once the pasta is ready, drain it and place the pasta into a medium-large pan over low heat. Add in the peas, Alfredo sauce, and mushrooms and gently stir to combine the ingredients.
6. Spoon the pasta into bowls and garnish with lemon zest, parsley, and chili flakes.

CRISPY QUINOA PATTIES

Burger patties are tough to come across for vegetarians and vegans alike. Restaurant options are quite limited in this aspect in regard to a variety of options. Usually the only options available are soya patties or Beyond Meatburgers. But at home the options are endless. These crispy vegan patties not only offer a fantastic boost of protein, they are also flavorful and crispy. Offering you a similar experience to fast-food burgers–but a much healthier option. You get to enjoy the flavor, comfort your cravings, and it's healthy? Sounds like a winning meal!

Difficulty Level: 7
Preparation Time: 45 minutes
Cooking Time: 30 minutes
Total Time: 1 hour 15 minutes

Nutritional Info Per Serving Servings: 4	
Calories	388
Carbohydrates	48.2g
Fat	17.6g
Protein	12.3g

Estimated Budget: $3.00-$4.00

Ingredients:

- 1 cup of quinoa (rinse and drain this a few times)
- 2 tsps of olive oil
- 1 tsp of cumin
- 1 tsp of garlic powder
- ½ tsp mixed herbs
- Salt to taste
- Zest of ½ a lemon
- ¼ cup of parsley

For the relish:

- 2 cups of cherry tomatoes, halved
- 1 cup of diced cucumber
- ¼ cup fresh basil
- ¼ cup of scallions, chopped
- 1 can of cooked chickpeas, drained and rinsed
- 3 tbsps of olive oil
- 3 tbsps of balsamic vinegar
- ½ garlic clove, minced
- Salt to taste

Instructions:

1. Place a medium-sized pot over high heat and add in the quinoa, 2 cups of water, salt, garlic powder, cumin, herbs, and olive oil. Stir the contents then bring to a boil. Cover the pot and reduce the heat

to low. Allow the contents to simmer for 20 minutes.

2. Make the relish while the quinoa cooks. In a medium bowl, combine all of the ingredients: tomatoes, cucumber, basil, scallions, chickpeas, olive oil, vinegar, cloves, and salt. Stir to combine.

3. Check back on the quinoa to see if the water has evaporated. If the quinoa is dry and has soaked up all of the moisture, stir it with a fork to break apart the grains. Add the lemon zest and parsley into the pot, stirring one final time, then remove it from the heat and set aside to cool down.

4. Once the quinoa has cooled, dampen your hands with some water and shape the quinoa into 4 equal-sized balls, then pat them down to hockey puck shapes. Place the patties on a plate and pop it in the refrigerator for 15 minutes.

You can prepare the cakes one of two ways:

5. Once the cakes are a bit firmer, remove them from the refrigerator and place them onto a saucepan over medium heat. Drizzle some oil into the pan and flip them over. Fry the cakes for about 5-8 minutes, until you notice a brown, crusted coat and then flip them over for another 5-8 minutes.

6. Alternatively, you can bake the cakes in the oven at 400°F for 20 minutes, but you won't get a crusted layer as much as the above option offers.

7. Place the quinoa cakes and top them with the chickpea relish and enjoy!

SQUASH STEW

The perfect home-cooked meal for winter is stew, stew, and more good ol' hearty stew! This recipe is a well-balanced combination of lentils, spinach, and squash, giving you a wholesome, spice-infused experience. Not only is it a wonderful immune boost considering all of those spices, this recipe also gives you a lovely natural boost of vitamins through its colorful array of vegetables. (If this doesn't sell it enough, just take a look at the nutritional table below.)

Note: this recipe makes use of a pressure cooker.

Difficulty Level: 3
Preparation Time: 15 minutes
Cooking Time: 35 minutes
Total Time: 50 minutes

Nutritional Info Per Serving Servings: 5	
Calories	325
Carbohydrates	57g
Fat	4g
Protein	19g

Estimated Budget: $4.00

Ingredients:

- 2 shallots, sliced thinly
- 1 tbsp of ginger, chopped finely
- 1 tbsp of vegetable oil
- 1 cinnamon stick
- 1 tsp of turmeric
- 1 tsp of coriander
- ½ tsp of fine cardamom
- ½ tsp of chili flakes (optional)
- 1 butternut squash, peeled and chopped into 1" chunks
- 1 lb of green lentils
- 6 cups of vegetable broth
- 5 cups of baby spinach, washed
- 1 tbsp of cider vinegar
- Parsley for garnishing

Instructions:

1. Get the pressure cooker ready and place it on medium heat. Add in the shallots, ginger, and a dash of oil; fry for 5 minutes until the shallots are a light brown, golden in color.
2. Pour in the coriander, cinnamon stick, turmeric, chili flakes, and cardamom. Cook for 1 more minute, stirring slowly to awaken the aromas.

3. Place in the butternut squash, lentils, broth and salt to taste. Cover the pressure cooker, lock it, and raise the pressure to high, then reduce the heat to medium-low. Let the contents cook for 12 minutes. You can release the pressure whenever necessary, by using the quick-release option.

4. After 12 minutes, add in the spinach and vinegar, and salt and pepper to taste. Stir for another 2 minutes. Garnish with parsley and serve warm.

Chapter Eight

DESSERTS & SHAKES

Welcome to party central! It only seems fair that the last chapter of this book on your favorite copycat recipes touches on the food that truly touches our hearts—sugar—and I'm talking lots of it!

If we're spending 2020 in isolation, what better way to spend that extra time at home, than to make sugary treats and shakes? We might as well...

This chapter's intention is to merely have fun and reap some sugary rewards in the process. Throughout this cookbook, a lot of the recipes took you around the world and through all of your famous drive-thrus; this chapter merely aims to get you exploring through your snack cupboard and see what desserts you can come up with.

The desserts that we've curated are the epitome of the phrase "short and sweet." Not only are they quick bites, but they're also easy ingredients to find in a pantry. You won't have to go to excessive lengths to find the 98% dark chocolate that's infused with salt from the Red Sea just to make a brownie. Thankfully, these recipes all require little to no cooking time and hardly any preparation. They're recipes that you can easily whip up and enjoy with not much added effort–the only time-consuming factor of the recipes will either consist of a setting time for the ice cream (to freeze) or baking a crust for a quick 10 minutes. You can always take these recipes and work them into bigger projects, i.e., adding one of the recipes to top off a cake that you baked. You could also make these small bite-sized desserts as a self-care gift for one of your friends by packing them into a small bag/container. The aim of this chapter, again, is to have fun and enjoy a treat while doing so.

We're going to start off by touching on a few treats that have grown quite popular over the past few years and then circle back to our own trend of traveling internationally, but from your kitchen, by ending off with a mystery dessert from a mystery location (don't look yet, you'll ruin the surprise!).

Other than our exciting finale dessert that's eagerly awaiting your perusal, we've included in these last few recipes Oreo truffles, which are similar to Italian kisses—but with a little twist: they have *actual Oreo* inside them. These cute, bite-sized balls are the perfect little treat for you, and they yield a glorious quantity of 16 truffles in one batch. The more, the merrier!

You'll also surely come across a few other deliciously adorable treats such as confetti squares and cookie dough and ice-cream sandwiches. All of these treats gained popularity as they became trends through social media a few years ago and are still as sugary and delicious as ever. Not only do these treats look cute and colorful, they're also delectable. The confetti squares consist of mini marshmallows, making each bite soft and sweet. The cookie dough and ice cream sandwiches are a creamy bite of heaven. If you're a fan of cookie dough, then this recipe is definitely a must-try for you. Lastly, we've got a deliciously thick and milky milkshake recipe, proper American diner style. All made from three simple ingredients at home!

OREO TRUFFLES

And we've reached *that* part of the book: the fun chapter! Here, we get to party! We're starting this chapter off with something simple and absolutely scrumptiously delicious—Oreo truffles. This 5-ingredient, bite-sized goodness is the best way to get any party started. Whether you're kicking back for a movie night indoors, or you're visiting a friend for their birthday, this snack can work its way into every occasion and everyone's hearts.

To spice things up, you can also add in your own twist on this recipe. A few options that you could play around with are to add nuts into the mixture; hard, crushed candy or even bits of marshmallow work perfectly also. If you're attending an occasion where there may be alcohol involved, you could even add a few dashes of drinks along the lines of Kahlua or Amarula into the mixture. This recipe is extremely versatile and will taste *amazing* either way.

Difficulty Level: 12
Preparation Time: 10 minutes
Cooking Time: 20 minutes (for freezing. No cooking required)
Total Time: 30 minutes

Nutritional Info Per Serving **Servings:** 12 truffles	
Calories	321
Carbohydrates	32g
Fat	19.9g
Protein	4.5g

Estimated Budget: $8.00

Ingredients:

- 1 pack of Oreos cookies
- 8 oz. of soft cream cheese
- 1 tsp of vanilla extract
- 2 cups of white chocolate chips
- ½ a cup of chocolate chips
- ¼ cup of chopped almonds (optional)

Instructions:

1. In two separate small bowls/mugs, melt the white chocolate chips and the chocolate chips in the microwave. Set them aside to cool.
2. While the chocolate cools, add the Oreo cookies into a food processor and pulse until they are fine crumbs. If you don't have a food processor, you can place the cookies in a plastic bag. Seal the bag

securely and then lay it on the counter. Use a rolling pin to smash the cookies until they're in smaller pieces, then roll it with the rolling pin until the fine crumbs are formed.

3. Get a medium bowl out and add 2 tbsps of the crushed Oreos into it, along with the cream cheese and vanilla extract. Stir well to combine the ingredients.

4. Prepare a baking tray (or a tray that can fit in your freezer) by lining it with a layer of parchment paper. If you have an ice cream scooper, make use of this to spoon out small balls of the cookie mixture and place them on the tray (if not–that's all right. Just use a tablespoon, but try to get them as round and ball shaped as possible).

5. Pop the tray in the freezer for at least 30 minutes so that the balls harden.

6. Dip the balls into the white chocolate, fully coating them. Then drizzle the other chocolate over the balls (create nice designs/patterns if you'd like to impress your guests a little more). Drizzle a few chopped almonds on each ball and then pop the tray back into the freezer for another 15 minutes.

COOKIE DOUGH & ICE CREAM SANDWICHES

It's safe to say that the 21st century has been taken over by ice cream sandwiches. These sweet and creamy delights took the world by storm when Instagram food trends started emerging, and thus, the chain stores who offer cookie and ice cream sandwiches have now graced our lives... and now we can't imagine a world without them! But thankfully we have the perfect recipe for when you've got those random cookies and ice cream cravings or if you have to entertain a few friends at your place.! This recipe is not only absolutely delicious with every bite taken, it's also super fun to make. If you find yourself bored at home one day, making a supersweet treat is always an option (and a really, really good one at that).

Note: Ice cream is a treat that's so extremely versatile in taste and texture. Be sure to adjust the ingredients to your preferred taste (as some may like a thicker, creamier vanilla ice cream while some might like a more peanut butter/toffee flavor, etc.). Try this recipe out first, if you want to get a hang of the method, then go ahead and experiment with your desired flavors.

Difficulty Level: 3
Preparation Time: 25 minutes
Cooking Time: no cooking required
Total Time: 5 hours 25 minutes (for freezing time)

Nutritional Info Per Serving Servings: 12	
Calories	376
Carbohydrates	48.2g
Fat	19.2g
Protein	4.3g

Estimated Budget: $6.00

Ingredients:

- 1 cup of butter
- 1 cup of packed brown sugar
- ¾ cup of sugar
- ¼ cup of milk
- 1 tsp of vanilla extract
- 2 ½ cups of all-purpose flour
- 1 tsp of salt
- 1 ½ cups of chocolate chips (some prefer shaved chocolate to this)
- 3 qt of soft vanilla ice cream

Instructions:

1. Prepare a baking tray (or a tray that will fit into the freezer) by lining it with parchment paper

(leave extra pieces hanging over the sides of the tray).

2. Melt the butter in a small bowl in the microwave. Let it cool down for a few minutes.

3. In a medium bowl, combine the melted butter, packed sugar, normal sugar, milk, and vanilla extract. Stir well to combine then add in the flour, salt, and chocolate chips.

4. Pour the dough into the tray, and press the dough down. Try to even it out as much as possible. Place a second layer of parchment paper over the top of the dough and place the tray in the freezer. Allow the dough to freeze for about 1 hour, so that it sets nice and firmly.

5. Once the dough is ready, place the tray onto the counter. Find the center of the cookie dough (widthwise) and cut down the center of it.

6. Using an ice cream scooper (preferably), scoop and layer ice cream onto the one half of the cookie dough.

7. Then carefully place the other half of the cookie dough layer (the one without ice cream) onto the other–so as to create the cookie and ice cream sandwich.

8. Pop the tray back into the freezer and freeze for at least 4 hours. Cut the cookie ice cream sandwich into small squares and serve.

9. Pro-tip: sprinkle some sprinkles or any of your favorite toppings on top of the sandwich to add more color.

CONFETTI BARS

Similar to the ice cream sandwiches, confetti bars have taken the internet by storm. Their cute, colorful marshmallow fillings are a visual depiction of the excitement that you experience with every bite you take. Whether you're just making these bars to treat yourself, or you're bringing them along as a snack to a friend's house–these confetti bars are a quick bite of literal joy and happiness!

Difficulty Level: 2
Preparation Time: 20 minutes
Cooking Time: 2 hours (mainly for freezing time)
Total Time: 2 hours 20 minutes

Nutritional Info Per Serving Servings: 16 bars	
Calories	411
Carbohydrates	40.9g
Fat	24.6g
Protein	8.4g

Estimated Budget: $5.00

Ingredients:

- 2 cups of chocolate chips
- 1 cup of peanut butter
- 4 tbsps of butter (preferably unsalted)
- ½ tsp of vanilla extract
- A pinch of salt
- 1 bag of mini rainbow marshmallows (10 oz.; if you can't seem to find mini marshmallows, you can use normal-sized marshmallows and chop them into tiny bits)
- ½ a slab of plain milk chocolate

Instructions:

1. Prepare a tray (one that can fit in your freezer) and coat it with a thin layer of cooking spray.
2. In a small/medium pan over medium heat, add in the peanut butter, butter, and chocolate chips. Stir the contents until fully melted. Once melted, turn off the heat and stir in the vanilla extract and a pinch of salt. Remove from heat and allow the contents to cool down to room temperature.
3. Once cooled, add the marshmallows into the mixture and stir well. Then pour the contents into the pan and level it out as much as possible. Place the tray in the freezer and allow it to set for up to 2 hours at least.

4. Once the bars are almost ready, get a bowl and a grater ready. Grate the ½ slab of plain chocolate (so that it's thin shavings).

5. Evenly sprinkle the shavings over the top of the tray's contents, then cut the marshmallow cake into small, bite-sized bars. Enjoy!

3-INGREDIENT CREAMY MILKSHAKES

Craving milkshakes happens more often than we actually make them. How often have you found yourself driving to a restaurant or drive-thru just because you craved a nice shake? The funny thing is that homemade milkshakes are really easy to make. It takes such less effort to make one than to actually go out and get one (not to mention the cost factor involved). You're also able to get super creative with your own homemade shakes, once you've got a basic recipe and method down. Here's a super simple look at an easy shake that you can whip up (pun intended) in a matter of no time. This recipe is a basic 3-ingredient shake, but feel free to add in your own twists (e.g., homemade caramel/toffee/chocolate sauce is a great option. Or you could simply top the shake off with some sprinkles and cherries—true American diner style!)

Difficulty Level: 1
Preparation Time: 10 minutes
Cooking Time: 0 minutes (no cooking required)
Total Time: 10 minutes

Nutritional Info Per Serving
Servings: 2

Calories	431
Carbohydrates	40.1g
Fat	27.5g
Protein	6.9g

Estimated Budget: $4.00

Ingredients:

- ⅔ cup of milk
- 2 cups of ice cream (flavor of the ice cream depends on the flavor you'd like)
- 3 tbsps of chocolate syrup (you can alternate this for something of your own preference)
- Whipped cream for the topping

Instructions:

1. Place the milk, chocolate syrup, and ice cream into a blender and blend until a smooth consistency.
2. Pour the contents into tall glasses and top with whipped cream. Add your own toppings if you'd like anything further.
3. Serve with a tall spoon/straw and enjoy!

BAKED MILK TART

In keeping with the creamy, milky desserts, it's only fair to add in the milkiest and creamiest of desserts: milk tart! This dessert has roots in the heart of South Africa. Mainly consisting of a thin, sweet pastry-crusted outer layer and filled with a custard filling, this dessert is sure to comfort that sweet tooth craving. It's decadently topped off with cinnamon powder, which perfectly brings all the flavors together. (The cinnamon part is very important, or else it will taste incomplete.)

Note: you will need a pie dish/tart dish that's oven safe and preferably has a removable base for this recipe.

Difficulty Level: 5
Preparation Time: 20 minutes
Cooking Time: 20 minutes
Total Time: 40 minutes

Nutritional Info Per Serving Servings: 6-8	
Calories	574
Carbohydrates	24.5g
Fat	28.9g
Protein	54.6g

Estimated Budget: $5.00

Ingredients:

For the crust:

- 1 ½ cups of all-purpose flour
- 1 ½ tsps of baking powder (or baking soda)
- ⅓ cup of castor/superfine sugar
- 3 oz of soft butter
- 1 egg
- A pinch of salt

For the filling:

- 2 cups of milk
- 1 cinnamon stick
- ¼ cup of white sugar
- 2 eggs
- 3 tbsps of flour
- 3 tbsps of cornstarch
- ½ tsp of vanilla essence
- 2 tbsps of butter
- ¼ cup of cinnamon to sprinkle on top

Instructions:

1. To prepare the crust, pour the flour, baking powder, and salt into a bowl and whisk until well combined.

2. In another bowl, mix in the butter and sugar and beat the mixture until it is fluffy (about 3 minutes); make sure that you don't overchurn the butter.

3. Crack the egg and beat it into the butter mixture, then slowly add the flour mixture into the bowl with butter and mix by hand, folding the contents into each other.

4. Prepare the tart dish. Place the dough into the dish and press it firmly around the edges. Pop the dish in the freezer for about 30 minutes.

5. Once the time is almost up, preheat the oven to 400°F and remove the tray from the freezer. Set it aside and allow it to warm up to room temperature.

6. When the tray has reached room temperature, place it in the oven to bake for about 15 minutes.

7. While the pastry is baking, place a small/medium pot over medium-high heat and pour the milk into the pot. Add in the cinnamon stick and bring to a boil.

8. In a separate bowl, crack the 2 eggs into it, and add in the sugar. Lightly beat the egg mixture then slowly add in the cornstarch and flour.

9. Pour the hot milk into the bowl and stir fast, then pour the mixture back into the pot. Stir the contents until thickened (almost custard-like in texture).

10. Once the mixture is thick, remove it from the heat and pour in the vanilla essence and butter. Continue stirring until the butter has melted.

11. Once the crust is ready (it should be a golden brown in color), remove it from the oven and pour the mixture into the crust.

12. Sprinkle the top with cinnamon and enjoy!

Conclusion

WHAT ONCE MAY HAVE SEEMED IMPOSSIBLE IS NOW POSSIBLE!

Y ou've done it! You've tackled some of your favorite dishes and explored the world with us. What an exhilarating and insightful journey it has been!

To start off on the most important question: did you manage to find the hidden Difficulty Level 10 gem? And did you try it out? Or are you planning on doing so? Let us know in a review on Amazon! We'd love to hear what difficulty level you started on and what you've leveled up to now. Let us know which countries and/or restaurants you visited on your journey here with us and what your favorite part of the experience was. Was there something unique that you learned through this read that you didn't previously know? We'd love to hear your thoughts!

Thank you again for choosing *Copycat Recipes* to not only be your cookbook guide but also your tour guide. Hopefully there are some fun facts about the recipes, their backstories, and their flavors that you also discovered through this read.

Don't forget to keep in mind all of the spices that you've used, as well as staple ingredients for your favorite meals—if you keep a good, constant stock of these long-life ingredients, then you'll soon find yourself saving big bucks. For example, if you found out that you enjoy a few dishes that consisted of oregano and baby spinach, try to keep stock of these ingredients as staple items so that you don't have to constantly buy more every time you need to cook. A little tip: these ingredients will also inspire you to further explore more dishes that have similar ingredients, or you might even find yourself experimenting with those ingredients in the kitchen, altogether.

If you find a sauce or even fresh produce that you enjoy, try to find out how long these items can be stored, preserved, or frozen, as this will also help you to make more of your favorite meals, while maintaining a healthy budget. Usually we forget to freeze items that might be getting old and completely ignore them until they're off—try to become aware of staple ingredients that you enjoy, and figure out how to promote the longest life for them, as this is when you'll find yourself cutting down on takeout, and cooking *even more* homemade meals!

Hopefully these tips have helped you to:

- gain/further your interest in cooking
- gain a higher understanding of meals and their history
- understand what makes your favorite meals so enjoyable (the spices, the flavors, etc.)

- understand the spices and juices that provide a unique signature of where the dishes have originated from
- heighten your skill set in cooking
- eagerly want to further challenge yourself in cooking
- overcome the fear/lazy factor that you might have had towards cooking homemade meals and realized
- save some money
- understand the ingredients and methods towards making your favorite meals (and hopefully bettering them) so they're as enjoyable as your favorite restaurant's meals!

Let's quickly reflect on the meals that we've touched on and take one key aspect from them.

With the Appetizers and Snacks chapter, we discovered the importance and role of what an appetizer is meant to fulfill. It's to line our stomach and prepare it for a main course meal, thus ensuring that we don't overeat in the process. What's more fascinating about this is that bread/carbohydrates are the best option for an appetizer, as it affects your taste buds the least, while still lining your stomach. What was your favorite appetizer/snack from the above chapter?

Next, we looked at vegetarian meals; we touched on the vast array of meal options that vegetables can create for us (especially burgers and sloppy joes). Did you try any of the recipes here, and which ones were your favorite?

We then moved onto fast-food inspired meals. The top five curated fast-food meals were heavily inspired by the culture of the United States, and we learned how to prepare a few of the favorite meals at home. Corn dogs, pizza pretzels and Wendy's chili are a few of the festive snacks/meals that you can easily prepare at home, for an any-time festive mood!

We then went onto the Italian cuisine and covered the trio of key ingredients, how they play a vital role in complementing each other, and how those ingredients are enhanced further, through the right spices.

Then we took a trip to Greece to uncover their amazing marinade and secret to tenderizing their meat. We also uncovered the spices that they use, as well as their signature use of olive oil and herbs.

We made a quick detour to Portugal and explored a variety of seafood dishes and their favorite piri piri sauce, not to mention making our own homemade piri piri sauce! We also discovered the benefits of the bay leaf and how it's incorporated into their cooking.

We then tackled a few vegan dishes from around the world: India, Thailand, and Italy. It's safe to say that the prominent flavors, spices, and aromas within each recipe offer a clear depiction of the origin of the dish.

Lastly, we covered a few treat options and explored the trends on social media, then finally kicked back and relaxed with an American diner-style milkshake.

We hope that this journey was fun and insightful for you and that you've learned a few key ingredients from different parts of the world, as well as how these ingredients play a part in the meals that you order from your favorite restaurants. Now you're able to make homemade versions, suited specifically to your taste, at a lower cost!

Hopefully you can now see how easy (and cheap) it is to travel the world, from the comfort of your own home. With a good enough challenge and a little backstory to kickstart your motivation for cooking, the world is your oyster! (Well, in this case, the kitchen is your world, which is then your oyster).

We thank you again for choosing *Copycat Recipes* as your choice of a cookbook and tour guide. Thank you again for coming on this journey with us. Hopefully, this read was insightful and motivating for you. Please do consider leaving a quick review on your experience, we'd love to hear from you!

Now that you've got all the tools in your hands, happy cooking and, once more for old time's sake and more importantly, happy eating!

REFERENCES

Abraham, L. (2019, October 23). *Dear spaghetti & meatballs, never ever change.* Delish.https://www.delish.com/cooking/recipe-ideas/recipes/a55764/best-spaghetti-and-meatballs-recipe/

Call, S. (2018, January 1). *Slow-cooked chili.* Taste of Home.https://www.tasteofhome.com/recipes/slow-cooked-chili/

Cheese-stuffed pizza pretzels. (n.d.). Tasty.https://tasty.co/recipe/cheese-stuffed-pizza-pretzels

Chef Rider. (n.d.) *Quick and easy pizza crust.* Allrecipes.https://www.allrecipes.com/recipe/20171/quick-and-easy-pizza-crust/

Cookie Dough Ice Cream Sandwiches. (2019, September 11). Delish. https://www.delish.com/cooking/recipe-ideas/recipes/a47405/cookie-dough-ice-cream-sandwiches-recipe/

Denney, S. (2018, January 1). *Indiana-style corn dogs.* Taste of Home.https://www.tasteofhome.com/recipes/indiana-style-corn-dogs/

Dolge, A. (2017, October). *Greek Chopped Salad with Grilled Pita.* Cooking Light.https://www.cookinglight.com/recipes/greek-chopped-salad-grilled-pita

Fatman. (2017, February 28). *MILK TART with a baked crust.* Food.com.https://www.food.com/recipe/milk-tart-with-a-baked-crust-530533

Fountaine, S. (2018, February 1). *Cilantro mint chutney recipe.* Feasting At Home.https://www.feastingathome.com/cilantro-mint-chutney-recipe/

Fountaine, S. (2018, February 18). *Frankies! (aka Bombay burritos) India's delicious street food.* Feasting At Home.https://www.feastingathome.com/indian-frankie-recipe/

Fountaine, S. (2019, August 9). *Crispy vegan quinoa cakes with tomato-chickpea relish.* Feasting At Home.https://www.feastingathome.com/quinoa-cakes-with-cherry-tomato-mint-and-chick-pea-relish/

Fountaine, S. (2019, October 18). *Chinese eggplant with spicy Szechuan sauce.* Feasting At Home. https://www.feastingathome.com/chinese-eggplant/

Fountaine, S. (2020, February 14. *Date night vegan alfredo.* Feasting At

Home.https://www.feastingathome.com/vegan-alfredo-sauce/

Giannopoulos, E. K., & Giannopoulos, A. E. K. (2020, April 13). *Gemista recipe (Greek stuffed tomatoes and peppers with rice)*. My Greek Dish.https://www.mygreekdish.com/recipe/gemista-stuffed-tomatoes-peppers-and-onions/

Giannopoulos, E. K., & Giannopoulos, A. E. K. (2020, April 27). *Marinated Greek lamb chops with roast potatoes (paidakia)*. My Greek Dish.https://www.mygreekdish.com/recipe/greek-lamb-chops-with-roast-potatoes-paidakia/

Gore, M. (2018, December 11). *Confetti squares is the dessert you didn't know you needed.* Delish.https://www.delish.com/cooking/recipe-ideas/a25440941/confetti-squares-recipe/

Gore, M. (2019, December 11). *Forget about a slice and grab a calzone.* Delish.https://www.delish.com/cooking/recipe-ideas/a26091626/easy-calzone-recipe/

Gore, M. (2020, April 30). *The antipasto salad to end all antipasto salads.* Delish.https://www.delish.com/cooking/recipe-ideas/a19885331/antipasto-salad-recipe/

HLSANDS. (n.d.). *Best ever jalapeno poppers.* Allrecipes.https://www.allrecipes.com/recipe/20858/best-ever-jalapeno-poppers/?internalSource=recipe+hub.

Holly. (2019, September 12). *How to make a milkshake.* Spend With Pennies.https://www.spendwithpennies.com/how-to-make-a-milkshake/

Jampel, S. (2019, November 3). *Spinach and feta tarte soleil.* Bon Appetit.https://www.bonappetit.com/recipe/spinach-and-feta-tarte-soleil

Karissa. (2019, January 23). *Vegan Worcestershire sauce.* Karissa's Vegan Kitchen.https://www.karissasvegankitchen.com/vegan-worcestershire-sauce/

Mendes, N. (n.d.). *Portuguese prawn cakes.* delicious.https://www.deliciousmagazine.co.uk/recipes/portuguese-prawn-cakes/

Miyashiro, L. (2020, January 2). *These Oreo truffles are just as delicious as they are easy.* Delish.https://www.delish.com/cooking/recipe-ideas/recipes/a48823/oreo-truffles-recipe/

Nagi. (2020, May 25). *Greek chicken gyros recipe.* RecipeTin Eats.https://www.recipetineats.com/greek-chicken-gyros-with-tzatziki/

Overhiser, S., & Overhiser, A. (n.d.). *Cauliflower tacos with yum yum sauce.* A Couple Cooks.https://www.acouplecooks.com/crispy-cauliflower-tacos/

Parisi, G. (2009, March). *Avgolemono chicken soup with rice.* Food & Wine.https://www.foodandwine.com/recipes/avgolemono-chicken-soup-rice

Portuguese fish stew (Caldeirada de peixe). (2019, April 26). olivemagazine.https://www.olivemagazine.com/recipes/one-pots/portuguese-fish-stew-caldeirada-de-peixe/

Portuguese prego with green piri-piri. (2018, May 11). olivemagazine. https://www.olivemagazine.com/recipes/meat-and-poultry/portuguese-prego-with-green-piri-piri/

Pressure Cooker Winter Squash and Lentil Stew. (2017, January 24). Good Housekeeping.https://www.goodhousekeeping.com/food-recipes/healthy/a42399/pressure-cooker-warming-winter-squash-lentil-stew-recipe/

Primavera skillet pizza. (2018, March 22). Delish.https://www.delish.com/cooking/recipe-ideas/recipes/a46837/primavera-skillet-pizza-recipe/

quotFoodThe Way To. (n.d.) *Portuguese Paella*. Food.https://www.food.com/recipe/portuguese-paella-226218

Ray, R. (n.d.). *Portuguese fisherman's shrimp and chorizo*. Food Network.https://www.foodnetwork.com/recipes/rachael-ray/portuguese-fishermans-shrimp-and-chorizo-recipe-2201002

Rege, L. (2020, March 17). *This is the easiest way to make chicken parm.* Delish.https://www.delish.com/cooking/recipe-ideas/recipes/a51451/easy-chicken-parmesan-recipe/

Saffitz, C. (2017, December 11). *Crispy cheese twists*.https://www.bonappetit.com/recipe/crispy-cheese-twists

Saffitz, C. (2018, September 18). *Broccoli and garlic-ricotta toasts with hot honey.* Bon Appetit. https://www.bonappetit.com/recipe/broccoli-and-garlic-ricotta-toasts-with-hot-honey

Sally. (2014, December 31). *Chicago-style deep dish pizza.*
Sally's Baking
Addiction.https://sallysbakingaddiction.com/how-to-make-chicago-style-deep-dish-pizza/

Schnitzler, J. (2018, January 1). *Crispy fried chicken.* Taste of
Home.https://www.tasteofhome.com/recipes/crispy-fried-chicken/

Smith, A. (n.d.). *Vegetarian sloppy joes.*
Allrecipes.https://www.allrecipes.com/recipe/163867/vegetarian-sloppy-joes/

Soy-braised chicken wings. (2019, November 19). Bon
Appetit.https://www.bonappetit.com/recipe/soy-braised-chicken-wings

Swasthi. (2019, September 22). *Paneer butter masala recipe,
how to make paneer butter masala.* Swasthi's Recipes.
https://www.indianhealthyrecipes.com/paneer-butter-masala-restaurant-style/

Woman's Day Kitchen. (2014, November 6). *Butternut
squash and kale torte recipe.* Woman's
Day.https://www.womansday.com/food-recipes/food-drinks/recipes/a11296/butternut-squash-kale-torte-recipe-124667/

Woman's Day Kitchen. (2020, May 27). *Chickpea, spinach, and quinoa patties.* Woman's Day.https://www.womansday.com/food-recipes/a32676061/chickpea-spinach-and-quinoa-patties-recipe/